The Baltimore Trail Book

Sierra Club, Potomac Chapter,
Greater Baltimore Group

The Baltimore
Trail Book

Suzanne Meyer Mittenthal

Revised Edition
Edited by James W. Poultney

Published by

The Johns Hopkins University Press
Baltimore and London

Maps by Milt Bankard

Second printing, 1993

The Johns Hopkins University Press
2715 North Charles Street
Baltimore, Maryland 21218-4319
The Johns Hopkins Press Ltd., London

Library of Congress Cataloging in Publication Data

Mittenthal, Suzanne Meyer.
  The Baltimore trail book.

  1. Hiking—Maryland—Baltimore Metropolitan Area—
Guide-books.   2. Trails—Maryland—Baltimore
Metropolitan Area—Guide-books.   3. Baltimore
Metropolitan Area (Md.)—Description.   I. Poultney,
James Wilson, 1907–   II. Title.
GV199.42.M32B345   1983   917.52'6   82–21216
ISBN 0-8018-2943-7

A catalog record for this book is available from the British Library.

Contents

Preface

The first edition of *The Baltimore Trail Book,* which appeared in 1970 and was reprinted in 1971 and again in 1973, was written by Suzanne Meyer Mittenthal and published by the Potomac Chapter of the Greater Baltimore Group of the Sierra Club. A revised edition is clearly needed. The original edition has for some time been out of print and copies are next to impossible to obtain. Moreover, during the past decade certain good hiking areas not included for detailed treatment in the 1970 edition have been developed with designated trails, to an extent that makes it advisable to include them in the new edition. Among several such areas two have been selected for inclusion: Soldiers' Delight Natural Environmental Area and Oregon Ridge Nature Center.

It is a pleasure at this point to acknowledge the great service performed by Mrs. Mittenthal and all who collaborated with her in the preparation of a book that has been so useful to lovers of the outdoors in the Baltimore area and so valuable in promoting respect for the importance of sound principles of conservation. Parts of the revised edition are repeated verbatim from the 1970 edition. On the other hand, certain changes have been made both in format and in the choice of what to include and what to exclude. In this edition the hikes, instead of being numbered serially throughout, are designated by arabic numerals under the separate chapters, which are also numbered. The addition of two new areas has made it advisable, for reasons of economy, to omit certain material that was included in the 1970 edition. The principal omission is the section on canoeing, which described eight areas, only two of which lie within Baltimore County. At the present time privately owned canoes can be kept at the Prettyboy Reservoir during the spring, summer, and fall by permit (telephone 795–6150), and canoes can be rented at the reservoir in Piney Run Park in southern Carroll County (telephone Carroll County Department of Parks and Recreation, 848-4500). Canoeing events are sometimes announced in the "Living" section of the *Sunday Sun* under "Living calendar."

Thanks are due to many persons who, through their good offices, have helped to make this book possible: to Sally Dieke and Martin Larrabee, who have been especially active in promoting the preparation of a revised edition; to Anneke Davis, Charles Davis, Betty Fisher, Steve Keplinger, Barbara and Martin Larrabee, Paul Meadows, John Railey, William Royer, April Storms, and Joe Sullivan, some of whom had written sections of the old edition and all of whom have written sections of the present edition. We are indebted to Milt Bankard, for map preparation, and to April Storms, for drawings illustrating some of the hazards to be avoided while hiking. We further owe our gratitude to all who may have assisted in the scouting of trails and whose names have not been formally recorded.

The editor and the Editorial Committee take this opportunity to express their gratitude to the Johns Hopkins University Press, for assuming the task of publishing this much-needed book and for providing the fine editorial services of Barbara Tilly. We are especially grateful to Arlene Sullivan, for her help in finding suitable authors for various sections of the book, for the time she devoted to bringing the manuscript to publishable form, and for her expert advice.

In order to make subsequent editions of *The Baltimore Trail Book* as accurate and up-to-date as possible, users of the guide are encouraged to send corrections, comments, or additions to text and maps to James W. Poultney, P.O. Box 31, Garrison, Maryland 21055.

MAP SYMBOLS

INTERSTATE HIGHWAY
ROAD
MAIN TRAILS
CONNECTING OR SIDE TRAIL
SHORELINE OF LAKE
RIVER
STREAM
WATERFALL
MARSH OR SWAMPY AREA
COUNTY LINE
POWER LINE
RAILROAD
ABANDONED MINE
BUILDING
CEMETERY
PARKING
REST ROOMS
RUIN
SCENIC OVERLOOK

Sykesville USGS Ellicott City

NAMES OF U. S. GEOLOGICAL SURVEY TOPOGRAPHIC QUADRANGLES COVERING AREA OF TRAIL MAP

MILT BANKARD
83

The Baltimore Trail Book

1. What You Can Do

The Book's Purpose

Many Baltimoreans do not know of the fine natural areas and hiking trails right in their backyard. The city's three reservoir watershed lands and metropolitan parks and the nearby county and state parks contain miles of trails in land as varied, scenic, and rewarding to amateur naturalists as any of the better known, more distant places in Maryland. Many more Baltimoreans do not know that the very existence of some of these nearby wild areas is threatened by the lack of desirable buffer zones, by poor planning for use, or by freeways. The only remedy is citizen involvement—increased public awareness of the areas and increased concern about policies that govern the lands.

The original edition of *The Baltimore Trail Book* and the present revised edition were written to alert Baltimoreans to the rich heritage of natural and scenic resources which has been preserved for them, and in the hope that, once informed, they will learn to enjoy and to take a greater part in preserving and protecting that fine natural wildlands heritage.

This book should not be without good effect on the wildlife of the parklands described here. It is hard for most people to accept that *all* natural objects must be left for others to enjoy, yet accept it we must in these times of population explosion. All uses of parks must be those that can be justified for all park users.

Public Officials to Approach

To begin to do your part in protecting and preserving natural scenic and recreational areas in Maryland, write to the agencies and officials listed below, indicating your interest in their programs and offering suggestions for the improvement or expansion of those programs. You can also join in the conservation work of one of the outing or conservation organizations listed in the next section.

1

CITY

Baltimore City Bureau of Parks, 2600 Madison Avenue, Baltimore, Maryland 21217; (301) 396–7900.

Bureau of Water Supply, Reception and Information, 2600 Madison Avenue, Baltimore, Maryland 21217; (301) 396–0259.

COUNTY

Baltimore County Department of Recreation and Parks, 301 Washington Avenue, Towson, Maryland. 21204; (301) 494–3871.

Baltimore County Executive, 111 W. Chesapeake Avenue, Towson, Maryland 21204; (301) 494–2450.

STATE

Maryland Department of Forests and Parks, Tawes State Office Building, Annapolis, Maryland 21401; (301) 269–3776.

The Governor of Maryland, State House, Annapolis, Maryland 21404; (301) 296–3901. Baltimore Office: 301 W. Preston Street, Baltimore, Maryland 21201; (301) 383-4950.

Outing and Conservation Organizations

Conservation and outing groups provide an opportunity to meet people who share your interests and who can often give valuable information about activities you may be interested in. Most of the groups listed below have memberships you can join to work on conservation matters related to your outdoor recreation interests. In the list below, however, conservation is given as an activity only if it is of primary concern to the organization.

By joining a conservation organization and becoming better informed about current issues, you can magnify the effect you have as a concerned individual in influencing events.

American Youth Hostels, Potomac Area Council, 1332 I Street, N.W., #451, Washington, D.C. 20005, (202) 783–4953. Emphasizes understanding people through travel and varied outdoor activities.

Baltimore Environmental Center, 333 East 25th Street, Baltimore, Maryland 21218; (301) 366–2070. Coordinates action on environmental matters and publishes the *Beacon,* a monthly news-letter announcing forthcoming events, including hikes.

Chesapeake Bay Foundation, Inc., 162 Prince George Street, Annapolis, Maryland 21401; (301) 268–8816. Promotes orderly management of the natural resources of the Chesapeake Bay and provides instruction in estuarine ecology, scientific investigation, and legal representation.

Deer Creek Watershed Association, Inc., P.O. Box 111, Darlington, Maryland 21034; (301) 836–3716. Promotes the conservation of the natural resources of the 135-square-mile watershed area.

Irvine Natural Science Center, St. Timothy's School, Stevenson, Maryland 21153; (301) 484–2413. Provides nature and conservation education, sells handbooks, and conducts field trips.

Izaak Walton League, Maryland Division, 6700 Needwood Road, Derwood, Maryland 20855; (301) 926–8713. National conservation organization.

League of Maryland Horsemen, Inc., Jeanne L. Long, 2005 Royal Gardens Drive, Baltimore, Maryland 21207; (301) 944–8963. Association of horseback riders.

Maryland Academy of Sciences, 601 Light Street, Baltimore, Maryland 21230; (301) 685–2370 (for 24-hour information, call 685–5225). Provides scientific education for visitors of all ages through live demonstrations and hands-on exhibits, daily scientific films, and the programs of the Davis Planetarium.

Maryland Conservation Council, Mary Ridgely Lang, corresponding secretary, 303 Kennard Avenue, Edgewood, Maryland 21040; (301) 679–9119. Association of Maryland outing and conservation groups; organized for the purpose of conservation lobbying in Maryland; represents and informs members.

Maryland Fly Anglers, c/o Norb Wagner, 3505 Gibbons Avenue, Baltimore, Maryland 21214; (301) 426–0840. Association of fishermen.

Maryland Ornithological Society, Inc., 4915 Greenspring Avenue, Baltimore, Maryland 21209; (301) 377–8462. Local and state organization to promote knowledge and conservation of wildlife and wildlife habitats; publishes *Maryland Birdlife* (quarterly) and *Maryland Yellowthroat* (monthly); lectures, field trips, etc.

Mountain Club of Maryland (MCM), Mrs. John R. Eckard, Jr., president, 4809 Roland Avenue, Apt. 2-B, Baltimore, Maryland 21210; (301) 467–7398. Maintains sections of the Appalachian Trail in Maryland and Pennsylvania; sponsors weekend and mid-week hikes for all ages through the year in the Baltimore area and in more remote areas.

Natural History Society of Maryland, Inc., 2643 North Charles Street, Baltimore, Maryland 21218; (301) 238–6116. Performs original research in the natural sciences.

Potomac Appalachian Trail Club, Inc., 1718 N. Street. N.W., Washington, D.C. 20036; (202) 638–5306 (evening only). (Open weekday evenings only.) Hikers' association; publishes Appalachian Trail guidebooks and maintains sections of the trail.

Sierra Club (Greater Baltimore Group), P.O. Box 135, Riderwood, Maryland 21139; (301) 477–0353. Active local conservation organization, with watershed lands, city parks, and work groups; sponsors outings.

Trout Unlimited, Inc., Barton F. Walker III, 1111 Park Avenue, Suite L-15, Baltimore, Maryland 21201; (301) 669–5070.

2. On Walking

From Exercise to Understanding

There are many reasons for going hiking—for exercise, for love of the wilderness, for refreshment of spirit, and for nature study. Although many of the trails in this book are short, on most of them you can realize these hiking objectives. Those who are accustomed to covering a great deal of ground in a day's outing may want to take two or three different hikes in the same area, while those who are less experienced or less energetic, who want to engage in detailed nature study, or who are accompanied by small children may prefer shorter hikes. The description of each hike begins with information on both the length of the hike and the ruggedness of the terrain.

The variety and intimacy of these trails should lead hikers to discover and to want to understand more of the fascinating life around them. A search for the great blue heron, the hickory horned devil, or the mad-dog skullcap, can be a much more rewarding wilderness experience than a casual hike taken only for exercise.

If you have no knowledge of nature in any form, perhaps the best way of learning to look and to see what is going on around you is to borrow at first from someone else's knowledge. This can best be done by going on hikes sponsored by some of the conservation organizations whose members are devoted to learning about the environment. Perhaps the best local examples of such groups are the Maryland Ornithological Society, the Mountain Club of Maryland, and the Sierra Club (Greater Baltimore Group). Members receive announcements of hikes, but non-members are generally welcome to participate in the hikes.

Nature study handbooks such as the Peterson guides are indispensable, especially to the novice. Field glasses and cameras are also most desirable. Carrying a guide minimizes the temptation to pick a plant for identification at home, and photographing the plant further reduces this temptation.

Handbooks

Learning to use nature handbooks or field guides is often the first step in developing an interest in some aspect of the natural environment. For many, the game of identification that field guides make possible leads to greater appreciation for and understanding of that environment. Information to help you move ahead in the game is contained in the field guides. Selected handbooks are listed below; all can be purchased at the Irvine Natural Science Center (see Chapter 1), which is open Monday through Friday from 12:00 to 4:00.

Borror, Donald J., and White, Richard E. *A Field Guide to the Insects*. Boston, 1970. $11.90.

Burt, William H., and Grossenheider, Richard P. *A Field Guide to the Mammals*. 3rd ed. Boston, 1976: $7.95.

Cobb, Boughton. *A Field Guide to the Ferns*. Boston, 1963. $10.95.

Conant, Roger. *A Field Guide to Reptiles and Amphibians*. Boston, 1975. $13.95.

Fisher, Alan. *Country Walks Near Baltimore*. Boston, 1981. $6.95.

Garvey, Edward B. *Hiking Trails in the Mid-Atlantic States*. Chicago, 1976. $5.95.

Henderson, Luis M. *Camper's Guide to Woodcraft and Outdoor Life*. New York, 1972. $3.50.

Klots, Alexander B. *A Field Guide to Butterflies*. Boston, 1951. $7.95.

McKenny, Margaret, and Peterson, Roger T. *A Field Guide to Wildflowers*. Boston, 1968. $14.95.

Murie, Olaus J. *A Field Guide to Animal Tracks*. 2nd ed. Boston, 1974. $9.95 hardcover, $6.95 paperback.

Peterson, Roger Tory. *A Field Guide to the Birds East of the Rockies*. Boston, 1980. $15.00.

Petrides, George A. *A Field Guide to Trees and Shrubs*. Boston, 1973. $9.95 hardcover, $6.95 paperback.

Pough, Frederick H. *A Field Guide to Rocks and Minerals*. 4th ed. Boston, 1976. $12.95.

Robbins, Chandler S.; Bruun, Bertel; and Zim, Herbert S. *Birds of North America*. New York, 1966. $7.95.

Thielcke, Gerhard A. *Bird Sounds*. Ann Arbor, 1976. $2.95.

Maps

Maps are essential for enjoyable and safe hiking. Sources of maps, including graphic maps such as those used as base maps in this book, are given below.

Topographic maps of each Maryland county (scale 1:62,500) are obtainable for $2 each from the Maryland Geological Survey, Rotunda Mall, 711 West 40th Street, Baltimore, Maryland 21211.

Statewide grid maps (scale 1:24,000) and general county highway maps can be bought from the State Highway Administration, Map Distribution Section, 2323 West Joppa Road, Brooklandville, Maryland 21022.

Many Maryland quadrangle maps are also available from Lucas Brothers Stationers, 221 East Baltimore Street, Baltimore, Maryland 21203.

Hiking Hints

To get the most enjoyment from hiking, you must be comfortable. Loose, durable clothing will be the least distracting. In cold weather it is better to wear several layers of clothing than one very warm one, so that you can peel off layers to adjust to your body's temperature as you warm with exercise and cool with rest. Long-sleeved and long-legged clothing is as desirable in warm weather as in cold; it serves as protection against poison ivy and brambles as well as dehydration and sunburn. Sturdy shoes and substantial wool socks are very important. A wide-brimmed hat is advisable, too.

If you find yourself hiking regularly, it will be worthwhile to invest in trail boots. A good pair of boots will protect your toes from rocks, support your ankles, and cushion the soles of your feet. Six inches is a good height. Boots should be roomy enough to allow your toes to wiggle. For further advice as to style, consult experienced hikers you meet on hikes sponsored by local outing organizations. Women may feel that hiking boots seem heavy in the store, but the support that good boots give on the trail far outweighs the negative effect of the added ounces.

One accessory that is essential in all seasons is a canteen; a small first-aid kit is also advisable. A poncho in your pack in inclement weather means that if it rains you can enjoy the storm. A small rucksack or an army belt-pouch is a fine investment for carrying lunches (and garbage after lunch), field guides, and poncho.

Map-reading skills develop fairly easily with practice. A compass is a great help in lining up the map with landmarks. The topographic maps used as base maps for trails in this book are United States Geological Survey quadrangle maps. Although contour lines are not shown on the maps in this book, they are indicated on the U.S.G.S. maps. Distances between contour lines on "quads" are twenty feet. The first and most important fact that hikers will learn in map reading is that contour lines close together indicate a steep slope, and far apart, relatively level land.

The chapters on the different areas give instructions on how to avoid getting lost, but one general precaution is in order: if you are not making a circuit hike, but intend to retrace your steps, be careful at crossroads and especially when you enter a road junction from one of the two arms of a Y-shaped fork, where there is danger that in returning you might take the wrong fork. In all such cases it is advisable to lay an arrangement of sticks in the form of an arrow pointing in the direction you are supposed to take.

3. Woodland Pests: From Ticks to Litterbugs

Poison Ivy

Poison ivy is the most common poisonous plant in eastern Maryland. It is easily identified, having a compound leaf with three leaves—known to botanists as *leaflets*—growing on one stem, and is usually found as an upright plant, in a trailing form on the ground, or as a vine on a tree. It flourishes everywhere, from deep moist woods to dry sunny hillsides, but is most frequently found growing along old fence rows and edges of trails and roadways. It is the hiker's constant companion.

The leaflets are variable in size, but are usually from two to five inches long and often notched. They are ordinarily a shiny dark green in color, but can vary from light yellow to red or scarlet, even in summertime. The leaflet at the tip has a longer stalk than those at the sides. Even when the leaves have fallen off, clusters of small white berries make identification of the vines easy. Vines in trees are connected to the ground by stems that are covered with aerial roots, thus giving the vines the appearance of thick brown ropes. There is no other common plant that resembles poison ivy, which has three leaflets and no thorns; Virginia creeper, like poison ivy in many of its growth habits, has five leaflets.

Most people are sensitive in some degree to poison ivy. Furthermore, immunity is unpredictable; no one is permanently immune; and everyone should avoid the plant. Poisoning is usually caused by contact with the plant. Merely brushing against one leaf may be enough to produce severe inflammation. The poison is easily transferred from one object to another—for example, from a dog or from clothing to the body. The poison is most virulent in the spring and early summer.

The best defense against poison ivy is to assume that it is everywhere, as in fact it is, and to look for it carefully before you stray from the center of the path. Wearing long-sleeved and long-legged clothing if you are going to be bushwhacking across fields or wandering in and out of the woods will enable you to enjoy

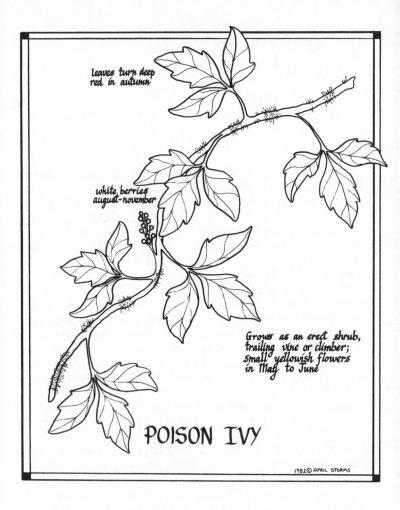

leaves turn deep
red in autumn

white berries
august-november

Grows as an erect shrub,
trailing vine or climber;
small yellowish flowers
in May to June

POISON IVY

1982© APRIL STORMS

yourself in somewhat greater safety. However, contaminated clothing must be washed separately and handled carefully to avoid spreading the poison.

Symptoms of poisoning may appear in a few hours or not until days after contamination. They include itching and subsequent inflammation and water blisters. Contents of the blisters are not poisonous, but poison remaining on the skin from the original contact may be transferred to another location if blisters are scratched.

Unfortunately, there is no absolute remedy for mild poison ivy poisoning. After suspected exposure, a thorough scrubbing with a strong soap (for example, laundry soap) or rubbing alcohol may help to remove the poison. Some simple commercial preparations may reduce the itching for some people. If inflammation persists for more than a few days or reaches sensitive body areas, a physician should be consulted immediately; relief is possible for severe cases.

Poison Sumac

Poison sumac grows as a coarse, woody shrub or as a small tree (never as a vine), most commonly in swamps and bogs. Its poisonous effects and treatment for them are the same as for poison ivy.

There are three common, harmless species of sumac which grow in the Baltimore area (generally in habitats hikers are more likely to encounter than bogs): staghorn, smooth, and dwarf sumac. The poisonous variety is easily distinguished from the nonpoisonous by its seedheads; the former has white berries, which hang in long loose clusters, whereas the latter all have red fruits, which are tightly packed and upright. Poison sumac leaves are also distinctive; they consist of seven to thirteen leaflets, arranged in pairs with the odd leaflet at the end. The leaflets are oval, have smooth edges, and are three to four inches long. Smooth and staghorn sumac leaves usually have more than thirteen leaflets with serrated edges. Harmless dwarf and poison sumac leaves are similar, but dwarf sumac leaves have a winged midrib (the stem from which leaflets grow has two short, projecting, leafy growths along its length).

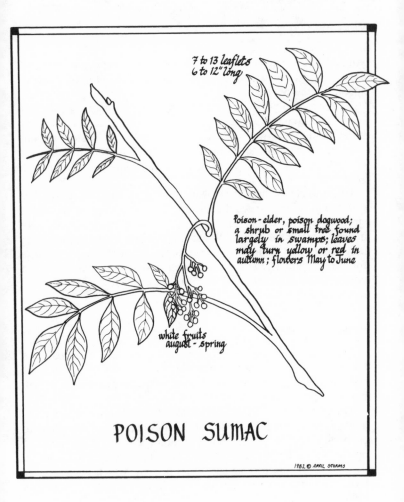

7 to 13 leaflets
6 to 12" long

Poison-elder, poison dogwood;
a shrub or small tree found
largely in swamps; leaves
may turn yellow or red in
autumn; flowers May to June

white fruits
august - spring

POISON SUMAC

1982 © APRIL STORMS

Ticks

Wood ticks are common in fields and low underbrush, in woods, and especially along paths. They can transmit rabbit fever (tularemia) and Rocky Mountain Fever and should be flicked off immediately when sighted on the body or clothing. Ticks are about an eighth of an inch long, round, and have eight legs; they have the appearance of a tiny, very flat crab. They do not attach themselves immediately, so do not become unnecessarily alarmed when you see one crawling up your leg. At the end of a hike, check all clothing before entering the car, and, upon reaching home, check once again in the privacy of your bathroom.

If a tick has become embedded, do not try to pick it off; the head may break loose, remain in the skin, and cause an infection. Get the tick to back out by applying a dab of rubbing alcohol, gasoline, kerosene, or vaseline. Wait a minute, until it can easily be detached, then dispose of it (do not attempt to squash ticks). Clean the bite with a disinfectant.

Chiggers

Chiggers are a family of mites. They are so small that most people don't know they have been bitten until the itching starts. Chiggers dwell in low, damp places, such as berry patches, woodlands, and grassy margins common to manicured public parks.

Preventive sprays and powders are available. If you are attacked by chiggers, kill them by washing them off as soon as possible with a thick lather of soap. Rinse and wash again. Apply antiseptic. Killing the mites does not stop the itching. No preparation but a local anesthetic, such as an ointment with benzocaine, is in any way helpful. Scratching may cause infection.

Snakes

The copperhead, a pit viper, is the only poisonous snake commonly encountered in the Baltimore vicinity. It frequents rocky, wooded areas. Its bite is seldom fatal, and it is one of the least aggressive of poisonous snakes; however, it should be treated with

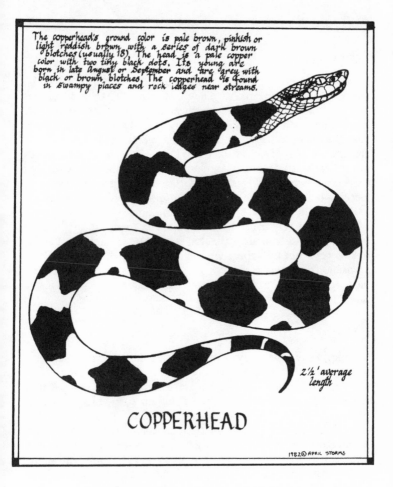

The copperhead's ground color is pale brown, pinkish or light reddish brown with a series of dark brown blotches (usually 18) The head is a pale copper color with two tiny black dots. Its young are born in late August or September and are grey with black or brown blotches. The copperhead is found in swampy places and rock ledges near streams.

2½' average length

COPPERHEAD

respect. Watch for the copperhead on warm, sunny days on rocky ledges; when climbing on a rock pile, never place your hands where you can't see them. Keep an eye open for copperheads on the trails, too. The snake's body is blotched with reddish brown spots; the head is a solid copper color.

To treat a snakebite, keep the victim immobile and apply a coolant to the wound to slow the circulation of venom. Get the victim to a physician as soon as possible.

Litterbugs and Flower Snatchers

Litterbugs and flower snatchers are two common woodland pests for whom education is the only possible remedy, and an infrequently effective one at that. Because some hikers might dig up rare orchids and other wildflowers we have not mentioned the precise locations of such plants in this volume. "Experts" are sometimes more insensitive than laymen to the need to leave all plants and blooms in place on public lands; perhaps they feel they are preserving rare specimens by transplanting them to their own gardens!

Most hikers are careful not to litter. It is a good idea, however, to devote a few minutes on every hike to cleaning up after the few who do, so that the trail will not be marred for all hikers.

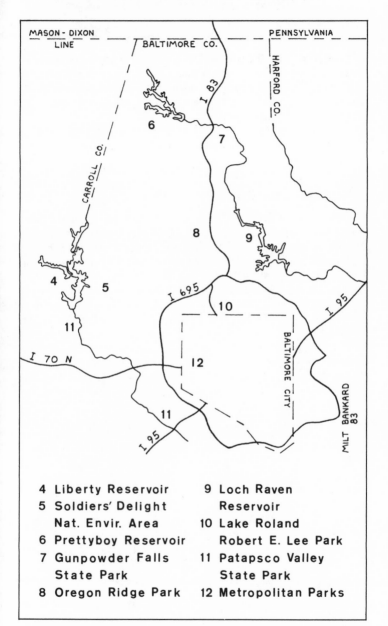

4 Liberty Reservoir
5 Soldiers' Delight
   Nat. Envir. Area
6 Prettyboy Reservoir
7 Gunpowder Falls
   State Park
8 Oregon Ridge Park

9 Loch Raven
   Reservoir
10 Lake Roland
   Robert E. Lee Park
11 Patapsco Valley
   State Park
12 Metropolitan Parks

16

4. Liberty Reservoir

Introduction to the Area

The Liberty Reservoir watershed area is a surprisingly varied and interesting region for hiking. Not only does it represent the natural characteristics of this locale, it also has some unusual features not normally found in this vicinity. At first glance, you would expect the area to be completely flat or, at most, gently sloping. However, some of the trails listed here are genuinely hilly. There are strong stands of deciduous growth, some of them hundreds of years old. Much younger forests are also represented, as are marshes, fields, pine forests, mixed forests, and some pine barrens. Veteran hikers, who now travel to the western Maryland, Virginia, and West Virginia mountains to find uncrowded areas, will be surprised by the seclusion of some of the trails listed here. In addition, there are a number of trails that offer a nice introduction to hiking for youngsters. Families will enjoy the shorter jaunts of just a couple of miles. There are also trails of 15 miles or more available to the most exercise-oriented hiker.

Liberty Reservoir, the newest of three Baltimore City–owned reservoirs, was created in 1954 by impounding the North Branch of the Patapsco River. Liberty Dam itself is a concrete gravity dam, with a crest at 420 feet above sea level. Of the 6,100 acres owned by the city around the reservoir, 4,664 acres remain in natural woodland. Much of the balance is planted in pines.

If you are looking for an area not far from home to hike in solitude, we think you will be pleasantly surprised by the Liberty Reservoir trail system. Keep in mind that not all watershed areas in this country are open to hikers; it is extremely important that we do not abuse this privilege. We have a responsibility not only to respect the land ourselves but also to protect it from misuse by others.

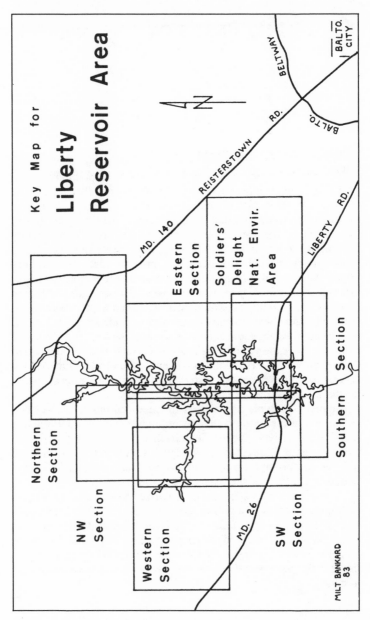

Key Map for
Liberty Reservoir Area

Northern Section

NW Section

Western Section

Eastern Section

Soldiers' Delight Nat. Envir. Area

Southern Section

SW Section

MD. 140

MD. 26

REISTERSTOWN RD.

LIBERTY RD.

BELTWAY

BALTO.

BALTO. CITY

MILT BANKARD 83

18

Regulations

Several regulations exist regarding the use of watershed lands, most of which are basic common sense. Pollution of the waters must be eliminated completely. Should no sanitary facilities be available, please use an area at least two hundred feet from all water, including potential water sources during runoff. Fires, motorized vehicles, ice-skating, and swimming are all prohibited, as is overnight camping. In addition, everyone should observe the hiker's golden rule: "Take nothing but pictures, leave nothing but footprints."

Access to the Area

Specific instructions for reaching the trail head are given for each trail described here. All are off Liberty Road (Md. 26) or Reisterstown Road (Md. 140), Baltimore Beltway (Interstate 695) exits 18 and 20, respectively. All can be reached in less than an hour from mid-city, even in bad traffic. Their easy access and proximity make them realistic trips at almost any time of day.

Getting Lost

If you get lost, do not panic. Liberty Reservoir can be seen from some portion of almost all the trails, making it easy to keep your bearings. Should you get off reservoir land, encroaching suburbia assures that help will never be far away. In addition, most of the trails are wide and difficult to mistake. It is a good idea, however, to be familiar with the surrounding area before embarking on your hike. Use common sense and enjoy yourself.

Hike 4.1 Morgan Run

Nine-mile moderate circuit hike, plus 1-mile (down and back) side trail to lake's edge; scenery ranging from open country to deciduous woods, several viewpoints, stream crossings, moderate to strenuous hill climbs; recommended in spring, summer, or autumn.

Trail's Attractions

Morgan Run Trail has some of the most varied scenery in the Liberty Reservoir area. The observant trekker will notice the quick succession of dense deciduous forest, open country, and pine forest. Suprisingly hilly, the trail offers pleasant overviews of the reservoir and quiet solitude along the banks of meandering streams. This is a nice day-hike for the seasoned wanderer, although it may be a bit strenuous for a family outing.

You will encounter water on the trail even in dry seasons. Therefore, this hike is not recommended in winter unless it is cold enough for the water to freeze. In addition, the trail is not enjoyable in snow, because of its frequent large hills.

Sections of Morgan Run Trail are fairly secluded, notably the far northern portion. This section bisects a dense forest before crossing the stream above Liberty Reservoir. Signs of civilization are apparent, however, along the first third of the trail, where it parallels the reservoir boundary for a short distance.

Wildflowers are abundant in spring and summer, including laurel, cinquefoil, daisies, big Mary bells, wild roses, and blooming strawberries and raspberries. Small mammals are common sights, along with fish, mallards, and reptiles (turtles and frogs, rarely snakes).

Diversity characterizes this trip. Bring all your senses and don't miss a thing.

Directions

To reach the starting point of Morgan Run Trail, take Liberty Road (Md. 26) west to Eldersburg (approximately 12 miles from Beltway Exit 18). Turn right at the intersection of Md. 26 and Md. 32 in Eldersburg. Proceed north on Md. 32, passing the Freedom Elementary School on your left. Turn left onto Irving Ruby Road, just beyond the school. Continue to the bottom of Irving Ruby Road. Park on the shoulder, so that you will not block the fire road.

The hike starts on the fire road. Follow it downhill for approximately a quarter of a mile. Turn onto the steep winding trail that forks off to the left. Should you miss this trail you will soon find yourself on the banks of the lake. Simply backtrack to the trail.

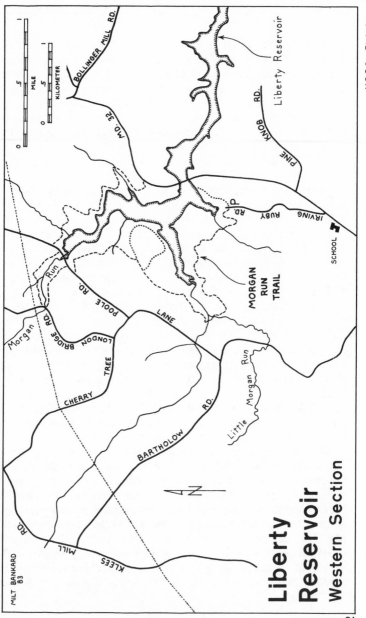

Liberty Reservoir
Western Section

MILT BANKARD 83

USGS Finksburg

21

After climbing the hill, the trail will level off as it winds in a northerly direction through a deciduous forest. It then crosses another fire road. Turn left onto the fire road; a right turn would lead you back down to the reservoir. Soon the road approaches the reservoir boundary, and a paved road becomes visible on the left. Continue along the fire road as it begins its descent to Little Morgan Run. You will probably have to wade or build a bridge across the stream here. It may be possible to use a large felled tree upstream as a bridge, but the necessity of bushwhacking back to the trail makes this choice questionable at best.

After traversing a planted section of strongly scented pines, the trail parallels the reservoir boundary. A few farms and houses are visible on the left. At the intersection of a gravel road, a trail juts off to the right, down to the edge of the reservoir. This trail is no more than a mile long, and the lakeshore is a good lunch spot.

Back on the fire road, continue to another fork in the trail. Take the path to the left and walk until you reach the intersection of the trail and a paved road (Poole Road). Turn right, and head back down toward the reservoir. At this point, no more than one hundred yards from the road, a small, inconspicuous footpath winds off to the left. It is easy to miss, so you may well find yourself down at the edge of the reservoir. This section of trail is worth searching for, however, so scrutinize the area before giving up and following along the reservoir up to Morgan Run. If you are successful in locating the trail, you will be rewarded with a beautifully serene stroll down to the stream. If the water is too high where the small trail crosses Morgan Run, continue up to London Bridge, a few hundred yards ahead, and backtrack to the trail.

After crossing a second, smaller stream, the trail leads up to the power line at the top of the hill. Follow the line to the second transmission tower, where the trail heads back into the forest. After leveling out again, the trail follows the reservoir, which will become visible again on your right. There is another stream to cross at the bottom of this hill. Follow the trail to the intersection with Md. 32. Turn right and cross the bridge. Much of the area just traversed can be seen from this vantage point. After crossing, look for a small footpath slightly above the drainage culvert. If this path is too difficult to follow, you can take any of the other trails that head down to the reservoir's edge. Follow the reservoir's shore around to the fire road and take the fire road back up to the car.

Shorter hikes and car shuttle hikes can also be taken on sections of the trail. For example, you can reach the upper section of the trail by continuing along Md. 32 to London Bridge Road just beyond the town of Gamber. Turn left onto London Bridge Road.

Hike 4.2 Abandoned Mine–Coot Peninsula

Hilly, winding, moderate trail, 5 miles one way, through deciduous and pine forest, out onto narrow peninsula; shorter hike possible.

Trail's Attractions

The Abandoned Mine–Coot Peninsula Trail is a very interesting walk that parallels the entire length of Liberty Reservoir. An early attraction of the hike is the old, abandoned chromite mine at the top of the first hill on the trail. The rock heaps include pieces of actinolite, mica, and asbestos. Even if you find the pit itself uninteresting, you should enjoy the view it opens up of the sur-rounding countryside.

After passing the mine, the trail continues to wind up and down through a pretty section of deciduous growth. Late spring is an especially good time to take this hike, because of the abundance of pink and white laurel in this section. Two miles or so into the hike, you will enter a section of planted pines, just after passing several fern-lined streams. The ferns give the woods a delicate, fragile appearance, highlighting this section of the trek. Keep your eyes open for wildlife here, as many animals are also attracted to these pleasant stream banks.

After following a wooded ridge, the trail drops down to water level as you walk out onto Coot Peninsula. In all seasons, the head of the peninsula offers a good view across the fingers of the lake. In late fall and winter, higher views are available at various points along the ridge.

The Abandoned Mine–Coot Peninsula walk is attractive because of its isolation. At any time of the year, it can give you a feeling of remoteness, in an area where solitude is no longer easy to find. This is especially true of the peninsula portion of the hike. Although the surrounding area is becoming more and more populated, with careful use we may be able to preserve this small piece of serenity.

Directions

The starting point of the Abandoned Mine–Coot Peninsula Trail is near the ending point of Hike 4.1, the Morgan Run Trail. Take Liberty Road (Md. 26) west to Eldersburg (approximately 12 miles from Beltway Exit 18). Turn right at the intersection of Md. 26 and Md. 32 in Eldersburg. Proceed north on Md. 32 approximately 2.5 miles, to the bridge over the reservoir. Park on the far side of the bridge. For those who wish to use a car shuttle system, continue on Md. 32 to Bollinger Mill Road, approximately 1 mile beyond the bridge. Make a sharp right hand turn onto Bollinger Mill Road. Continue until the road dead-ends against reservoir property. Be careful not to park your car where it will block the fire road.

The hike from Md. 32 to Coot Peninsula and back is just under 10 miles. If you use the car shuttle method, the distance from Md. 32 to Coot Head and then back to Bollinger Mill Road is approximately 6.5 miles. Should you really be pressed for time, the easy jaunt from Bollinger Mill Road down to Coot Peninsula and back is approximately 3.5 miles. For a longer hike, try combining this trail with Hike 4.3, the Middle Run Trail.

The trail entrance on Md. 32 is wide and easy to locate. When you reach the first trail intersection at the top of the hill, take the branch to the left. The old, abandoned mine is just a few feet farther. Continue on the main trail through the woods to the pine plantings and, at the next intersection, take the trail to the right. This trail follows an underground electric line along the ridge. You will see the reservoir on your right. After descending, watch on your left for a small path that ascends the hill; if you miss it, you will end up at the reservoir's edge. Ascend this small path up to the main trail and turn right to Coot Peninsula. When returning, if you used the car shuttle method, continue straight on this trail until you reach Bollinger Mill Road. To return to Md. 32, you can continue on this trail past the small path used earlier to ascend the hill. Turn left onto the next trail, a wider one that will also return you to the main trail. This will give you a change of scenery on the way back.

Hike 4.3 Middle Run–Piney Point

Six and one-half mile, easy-to-moderate circuit hike through forest and some marsh area; good birding area; shorter loops also available; recommended in spring, summer, and fall.

Trail's Attractions

The Middle Run area offers diverse scenery, some of which is not available anywhere else in the Liberty Reservoir vicinity. The marsh area on either side of Middle Run is an especially surprising contrast to the surrounding area. In addition, portions of the forest in this region include both pines and deciduous growth. In other areas around the reservoir, these varieties are almost always segregated. The two peninsula portions of this trail travel through thick pine forest, the fallen needles providing a soft, quiet walkway in all seasons. There are frequent stream crossings on parts of this trail, so a winter trek could be a bit frosty on the toes. Since the area includes an open field surrounded by deep woods, you should see a wide variety of birds on your hike. In addition to many kinds of perching birds, you may also have an opportunity to view red-tailed hawks.

Overall, the trail makes for an interesting day trip, in pleasant and relatively secluded surroundings. You are most likely to encounter other people on the trail to Piney Point, or on the section along Deer Park Road. The Deer Park Road access is used heavily by local teenagers, but hiking a mile or so on the trail should put you beyond almost everyone. If you do not have time for the entire trip, try the hike from Deer Park Road to one or both of the peninsulas. If you are more intrigued by the marsh area, eliminate Piney Point. A few other shortcuts are mentioned in the directions for those who find that they have spent too much time in one area.

Directions

You can begin the circuit hike at one of two locations. The first is at the end of Bollinger Mill Road. (See Hike 4.2 for directions to Bollinger Mill Road.) Begin your hike from this access point by taking the fire road on your left at the end of the road. Continue by

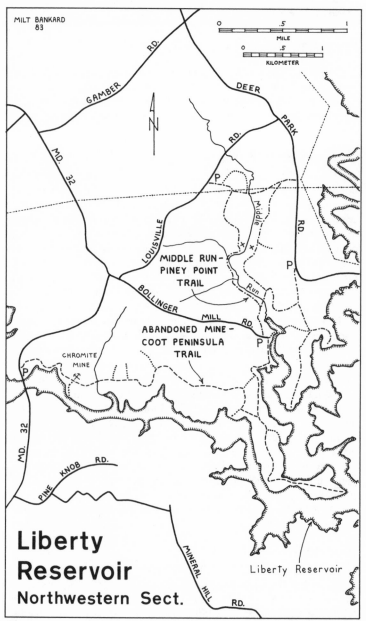

MILT BANKARD
83

GAMBER RD.

DEER PARK RD.

MD. 32

LOUISVILLE RD.

BOLLINGER

MILL RD.

Middle Run

P

P

P

P

MIDDLE RUN–
PINEY POINT
TRAIL

ABANDONED MINE–
COOT PENINSULA
TRAIL

CHROMITE
MINE

PINE KNOB RD.

MINERAL HILL RD.

Liberty Reservoir

Liberty
Reservoir
Northwestern Sect.

USGS Finksburg

following the directions given below, starting after the trail reaches Bollinger Mill Road. Shorter circuits are available by crossing Middle Run in a number of places and returning back to Bollinger Mill by walking south back to the marsh area.

The second access is on Deer Park Road. To reach Deer Park Road, take Reisterstown Road (Md. 140) from the Beltway (Exit 20) and go north (toward Reisterstown). Seven miles from the Beltway, make a left onto Berryman's Lane (if you pass Chartley Shopping Center on the right you have gone too far). Take Berrymans' Lane to the first intersection and make a right onto Nicodemus Road. Nicodemus Road will turn into Deer Park Road after it crosses Ivy Mill Road. Pass over the reservoir bridge and travel 1 mile to the trail head. There will be a large parking area on the left. The entrance is marked by a fire road sign.

Early in your hike (starting at the Deer Park Road access) you will notice mulberry trees, raspberry bushes, honeysuckle, and wild rose. It is not difficult to understand why birds are so attracted to this area. Approximately half a mile from the trail head, you will come to a three-way intersection of fire roads. Continue straight to Piney Point, take the middle route out to the peninsula, or turn sharply to the right to head down to Middle Run. Both peninsula walks are worth taking, but you can expect fewer people on the longer walk (middle fork).

Return to the three-way intersection after you have explored the peninsula to your satisfaction. Take the fork leading to Middle Run. The trail will give you the impression that you are walking in a stream bed. Follow it to the open field and the old bridge abutment. (The easiest place to cross Middle Run here is by bushwhacking to the right near the large rock outcropping on the other side of the stream. The water is shallow enough just above this outcropping to cross easily almost year-round.) Follow the rock outcropping up to the other side of the fire road. You may want to spend some extra time in this unique area before you continue your trip. When you reach Bollinger Mill Road, turn on the fire road to the right. (If you are beginning your hike here, turn left on the fire road and continue as indicated below). Follow Middle Run by taking the right fork when the trail splits north of Bollinger Mill Road. After the trail descends to stream level, you have the option of crossing over and cutting your hike short (see XXX markings on the map). For the longer circuit, continue north along the tumbling stream, cutting through a pretty piece of forest. After crossing a very small stream, you will be able to ford Middle Run again.

After crossing Middle Run, follow the trail up the hill (not to the right along the stream). Another shortcut can be taken by turning on the next trail on your right, following it up the hill and back to the main fire road (turn left onto the main fire road back to Deer Park Road). To cover the entire circuit, continue straight, crossing the stream and ascending the next hill. This trail will eventually lead out to Louisville Road, so turn right onto the first trail after you ascend the hill and travel back down to stream level again. Soon thereafter, you will come to the main fire road again. Turn left and go up to Deer Park Road. Turn right onto Deer Park Road and go .3 mile down to the parking area.

A longer hike can be made by combining the best parts of this trail with Hike 4.2, where the two meet at Bollinger Mill Road. The entrance to Middle Run from Louisville Road is not recommended, since a portion of the property is owned by the Baltimore Gas and Electric Company.

Hike 4.4 Keyser Creek

Easy 3.5-mile circuit or 3-mile, one-way hike through wooded area; recommended in all seasons.

Trail's Attractions

Keyser Creek runs into Liberty Reservoir in a rocky, steep-sided cliff area. Consequently, this trail offers easy climbing and a much higher viewpoint than most of the Liberty Reservoir trails. The woods contain a variety of deciduous growth, including some old stands of oak and hickory. The trail also passes sections of pine plantings. This area is ideal for wildlife; unfortunately, it must support more than its share as a result of the unchecked growth of the neighboring suburbs.

Due to its proximity to Reisterstown, the Cockeys Mill Road end of the trail attracts many people. Most of them, however, spend their time down at the reservoir itself, so you may not even be aware of them on your hike. The trail has one other flaw: traffic noise from Md. 140. It can be heard from almost every section of the path, making it difficult to forget where you are. In the mornings and evenings, thousands of birds congregate in a section of pines near the north end of the loop. They do their utmost to drown out the traffic noise; sometimes they almost succeed.

We recommend Keyser Creek in the off-season, or as a family outing to introduce youngsters to the forest.

Directions

The Keyser Creek Trail is easy to follow in either direction. You may begin at the end of Cockeys Mill Road or on Md. 140, just south of the bridge that crosses this narrow part of Liberty Reservoir. Cockeys Mill Road becomes a dirt road at its end, so it may be better to start from Md. 140 on rainy days. You can use the loop section of the trail to return to your original parking place, or you may arrange a car shuttle at each end.

To reach Cockeys Mill Road, take Reisterstown Road (Md. 140) from the Beltway (Exit 20). Go north toward the town of Reisterstown. Cockeys Mill Road is approximately 7.5 miles from the Beltway, on the left-hand side. If you pass Franklin Junior High School or the Reisterstown Volunteer Fire Department, you have gone too far. Follow Cockeys Mill Road for approximately 3 miles to its end. Park in the open dirt area, being careful not to block the fire road.

Begin your hike on the fire road to the right. (Do not follow the trail that leads straight down from Cockeys Mill Road; it goes to the reservoir.) Walking along the fire road, you will come to a stream crossing in less than half a mile, followed soon by the loop portion of trail. To the right, the trail goes along a ridge; to the left, it runs closer to the reservoir. Not even from the ridge trails, however, are there any good views of the reservoir. A second small stream crossing occurs on the opposite end of the loop. This brook is more scenic than the first, since it includes some cascading water in most seasons.

The foliage is denser on the northern portion of the trail (the Md. 140 end). Unfortunately, the traffic noise at this end is louder than

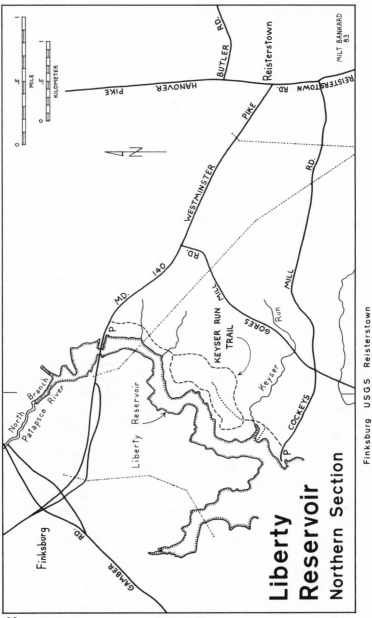

Liberty Reservoir
Northern Section

Finksburg USGS Reisterstown

that near Cockeys Mill Road. You may find deer tracks on this portion of the trail, possibly even on the ridge directly over Md. 140.

If you choose to begin your hike on Md. 140, travel approximately 10.3 miles north on Reisterstown Road from Beltway Exit 20. (Be sure to bear left in the town of Reisterstown to stay on Md. 140.) The entrance to the trail is on the left, approximately one hundred yards before you reach the bridge. The trail runs up the hill and is marked by a fire road sign. It leads away from Liberty Reservoir and runs parallel to Md. 140.

Hike 4.5 Oakland

Moderate 6.5-mile hike (one way, including two spurs); or easy 3.5-mile circuit (including some road hiking); varying scenery including good views of the reservoir in many locations; recommended in all seasons.

Trail's Attractions

The Oakland Trail offers enjoyable hiking in a fairly quiet area, with frequent pleasant views of Liberty Reservoir. The scenery is markedly different on opposite sides of Oakland Road. For most of the southern section, from Ward's Chapel Road to Oakland Road, the trail runs along a ridge in a section of forest very representative of the dominant growth patterns in this area. There are few pines, but large stands of fine hardwoods in a mature forest do exist. The reservoir views that can be glimpsed through the deciduous growth in this area are enjoyable even in the height of summer. In autumn, this section of trail is one of the best in this area. The southern portion of the trail is also more effectively isolated from the intrusions of man than are other sections.

The Oakland Road area has a character all its own. An old water wheel serves as backdrop for the cascading stream that feeds the reservoir here. This is one of the many attractive lunch spots on the trip.

The northern portion of the trail offers more diverse scenery, and, in some areas, better animal habitats. For example, you are probably more likely to see deer in the middle section of this trail

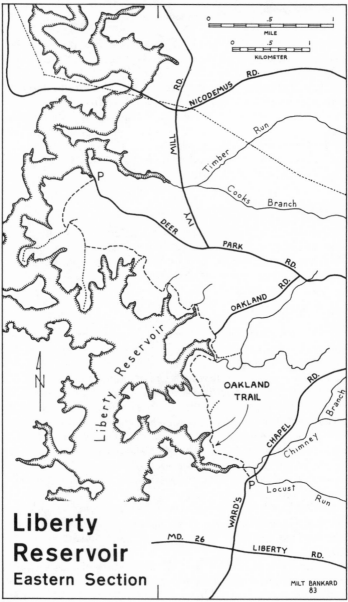

MILE

KILOMETER

NICODEMUS RD.

MILL RD.

Timber Run

Cooks Branch

IVY

DEER PARK RD.

OAKLAND RD.

P

Liberty Reservoir

N

OAKLAND TRAIL

CHAPEL RD.

Chimney Branch

Chimney Run

P

Locust Run

WARD'S

Liberty
Reservoir
Eastern Section

MD. 26

LIBERTY RD.

MILT BANKARD
83

than anywhere else in the Liberty Reservoir vicinity. The north-ernmost portion of trail is marred by encroaching suburbia; how-ever, the spur trails should not be missed. Covered with pine needles, these walkways offer excellent overviews of the reservoir. Although each has its own unique characteristics, they are gen-erally similar. One of the two may be eliminated if you are pressed for time.

Directions

To reach the entrance on Deer Park Road, take Liberty Road (Md. 26) west 5 miles from Beltway Exit 18 to Deer Park Road. Turn right just beyond Deer Park Plaza Shopping Center. Follow Deer Park Road approximately 6 miles to its end. Along the way you will pass an access road to Soldiers' Delight (see chapter 5 for details on this area). There is plenty of parking at the end of Deer Park Road; be careful not to block the fire road. To start your hike, take the left fork of the fire road when entering the woods.

To find the Ward's Chapel Road entrance, take Liberty Road west approximately 6 miles from Beltway Exit 18 and turn right onto Ward's Chapel Road. Follow for .6 mile to the bottom of the hill, where there will be a small paved driveway on your left. There is plenty of room for parking on the road shoulder. To begin your hike, walk up the driveway beyond the bridge over Locust Run. Watch carefully on the left for the trail entrance. The trail, small and covered with grass at its origin, soon becomes wider. It follows Locust Run for a short distance before turning north. It is easy to follow as it travels along this pretty ridge. A little over a mile from Ward's Chapel Road, you will come to the first trail intersection. Continue straight. The trail then winds down to the edge of the reservoir and the intersection with Oakland Road. Turn left on the gravel road that runs above the reservoir and follow it to its junction with Oakland Road. A fire road then turns to the left and heads up the hill (Oakland Road is visible straight ahead). Follow the fire road for approximately three-quarters of a mile. Take a sharp left on the trail that comes up from the direction of the reservoir. (The trail straight ahead here is the unnamed road shown on the map; it soon intersects Deer Park Road.) Soon after turning left here, you will come to another intersection. If you like, you can take the fork to the left here for a side trip down to the reservoir. Beyond this fork, the main trail borders the reservoir property. A few houses will be visible on your right. In spite of these, the spur trails, which soon come up on your left, are quiet and peaceful. After returning from any of the side trips you may have taken, continue up the main trail to the intersection with Deer Park Road.

If your time is limited or you find a car shuttle system impractical, you may want to try the short circuit from the end of Deer Park Road to the unnamed road and back. To complete this circuit, you will have to walk along Deer Park Road and South Lake Way back to the car.

If you are looking for a longer hike, combine this trail with Hike 4.6, Ward's Chapel Trail, which follows.

Hike 4.6 Ward's Chapel

Easy, peaceful, 3.5-mile circuit hike, or horseshoe-shaped shuttle hike of 2.5 miles.

Trail's Attractions

This is a flat, meandering trail that follows Locust Run before turning to pass through deciduous woods and native white pines. In the first half mile of trail, there are many side paths on the right, leading down to Locust Run and to Liberty Reservoir. Many of the coves they lead to are ideal for duck-watching or restful contemplation. On this trail, as on many others in the Liberty Reservoir area, you may occasionally see deer.

Ward's Chapel Trail is very close to Liberty Road, but its feeling of seclusion will surprise you. It is especially enjoyable for a winter hike, or for a quiet stroll on a late spring or summer evening. The sun's reflection on the stream and lake, shimmering through the woods, brings the trail to life. In April and May, dogwood and tulip trees are in bloom near the path; laurel follows in early June.

The Ward's Chapel hike is unusually relaxing, a great way to unwind or clear the cobwebs from your head. It also makes for an enjoyable family outing, even with small children.

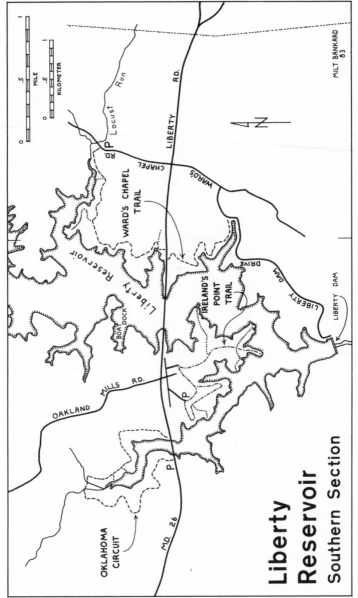

Liberty Reservoir
Southern Section

OKLAHOMA CIRCUIT

OAKLAND MILLS RD.

WARD'S CHAPEL TRAIL

IRELAND'S POINT TRAIL

Liberty Reservoir

BOAT DOCK

LIBERTY DAM DRIVE

LIBERTY DAM

Locust Run

CHAPEL RD.

LIBERTY RD.

WARDS RD.

MD. 26

MILE

KILOMETER

MILT BANKARD 83

Finksburg USGS Reisterstown

Directions

Follow Liberty Road (Md. 26) west approximately 6 miles from Beltway Exit 18 to Ward's Chapel Road. (Ward's Chapel Road is west of Randallstown and east of the first bridge across Liberty Reservoir on Md. 26.) Turn right onto Ward's Chapel Road and travel approximately .6 of a mile to the bottom of the hill, where there will be a small paved driveway on your left. Park on the shoulder of Ward's Chapel Road.

The trail is not a true circuit hike, as you must leave the woods and follow Ward's Chapel Road for approximately a mile to get back to the car. You can avoid this by parking a second car in the first parking area on Liberty Dam Drive. (Turn left onto Ward's Chapel Road from Liberty Road and watch for the Liberty Dam entrance, approximately three-tenths of a mile on your right.) However, since the hike is short, the extra distance added by the trek on Ward's Chapel Road is not unpleasant.

Begin your hike by walking down the driveway and turning left onto the fire road you will soon see. The trail is marked by the Bureau of Engineering's famous No sign, prohibiting everything on reservoir property but walking. Keep in mind that in many parts of the country reservoir property is marked by an even more restrictive posting, No Trespassing. Fortunately, this has not yet become necessary in Baltimore County. The trail meanders through the woods, rolling gently to the southwest. Approximately a quarter of a mile into the trip, you will notice the first of the small side trails mentioned earlier. This one leads down to Locust Run. Since this is a short hike, you should have an opportunity for a little exploring on some of these trails.

Continuing along the main fire road, you will come to an abandoned paved road about 1.5 miles into the hike. Follow it downhill, almost to the water's edge. On the left, just beyond a barely discernible stream, a path leads up through the trees. Follow this path to Liberty Road. Cross the road and walk approximately one hundred yards to the right, where the fire road will appear. Cut back into the woods on the fire road. The trail is easy to follow for about the next mile, until its intersection with Liberty Dam Drive. Turn left on Liberty Dam Drive and follow it to the intersection with Ward's Chapel Road. Turn left onto Ward's Chapel Road and return to the car. If time allows, you may wish to return by way of the trail.

Hike 4.7 Ireland's Point

Four and one-half mile easy round trip, including many side spurs to the reservoir's edge; through deciduous growth and pine plantings; recommended in all seasons; several shorter hikes available.

Trail's Attractions

Ireland's Point Trail is a peaceful, leisurely trek that leads to a number of peninsulas on the reservoir. It is named for some of the original inhabitants of this area. There are few hills and the walking is easy the entire way. The hike can be stretched to more than 4 miles if you visit all four points going out from the main peninsula and take the first side trip, a short jaunt to the edge of the reservoir. A bald eagle was spotted in this area in the spring of 1982, so, although you may not expect it to be a haven for wildlife, it would be wise to keep all your senses finely tuned.

Unfortunately, the trail is close to Liberty Road, and traffic noise is an obvious detriment. The most distant points, however, have a certain feeling of isolation. They also make good spots for picnics. You can see the Liberty Road bridge from the first point on your left. In very dry weather, you may also be able to walk nearly to the middle of the reservoir from this point.

Perhaps the best time to try Ireland's Point Trail is on a summer evening, or an autumn afternoon.

Directions

To reach Ireland's Point Trail, take Liberty Road (Md. 26) west from the Beltway (Exit 18) and travel 8.7 miles to Oakland Mills Road, the first left-hand turn west of the first bridge on Liberty Road. Turn left onto Oakland Mills Road and then make an immediate right onto Old Liberty Road. Follow this for a short distance to Mellor Avenue, a gravel road on the left. Travel to the end of Mellor Avenue, being careful not to park on the private property here. To reach the trail's entrance, which is marked by a No sign, you must cross private property. The owner has been gracious enough to allow access to hikers across his land. Please do not abuse this privilege.

When you enter the woods, take the first trail to the left. The next fork to the right leads down to the edge of the reservoir and is no more than a quarter of a mile long. Return to this intersection after your side trip and take the other fork down to the peninsula. After passing an open field on your left, the trail will run by a residence, also on your left. It then turns right, leading down to the four points. As noted earlier, the Liberty Road bridge can be seen from the first point on the left. If this view is not what you consider scenic, try scanning the bank on the opposite side of the reservoir. You may be able to spot Liberty Dam Drive, near the place where the Ward's Chapel Trail ends (see Hike 4.6). The most isolated of the four points is probably the one to your right off the main trail. It overlooks the area of the reservoir also seen from the reservoir's edge at the end of your first side trip. Ireland's Point itself (straight ahead on the main trail) offers the widest view of the reservoir. Liberty Dam can be seen from here, off to the left. Return to your car by retracing your route.

Hike 4.8 Oklahoma Circuit

Easy, wooded, two and one-quarter mile circuit; recommended in all seasons.

Trail's Attractions

The Oklahoma Circuit is easily accessible and offers a pleasant stroll at any time of year. Short in length, it features easy stream crossings, a few moderate hills, nice stands of deciduous growth (especially maples), and a variety of wildflowers and mosses. There are no direct views of the reservoir from the trail itself, but a few footpaths run to the water's edge.

The major drawback of the trail is encroaching suburbia. Backyards border the trail on the left during many portions of the hike. You may feel you have really reached the end of the line when you see a cemetery on your left near the end of the trek. Surprisingly, however, traffic noise is usually less of a distraction here than it is, for example, on Hike 4.7, Ireland's Point.

The Oklahoma Circuit is a good exercise trail. It also suits those on a limited time schedule, since the car is never far away. In case of emergency, the proximity of a nearby home can also be an advantage.

Directions

The Oklahoma Circuit hike starts at the west end of the second bridge on Liberty Road (Md. 26). Travel approximately 9.5 miles west of Beltway Exit 18 to the second bridge. Park on the shoulder of Liberty Road. The entrance to the trail is at the end of the metal railing on the west side of the bridge. The path is very narrow at the beginning, but it soon widens. Follow it away from the reservoir. Approximately half a mile into your hike, you will come to an intersection with a large grass pathway. A pipeline runs underneath this pathway. You may either continue straight on the main trail or turn right onto the pipeline. Since the trail has a not-so-interesting backdrop of nearby homes, you may prefer to follow the pipeline, even though its pathway has more hills than the regular trail and you are also more likely to see that other product of suburbia, the motorbike. Should you decide on this option, follow the pipeline for less than half a mile, until it intersects again with the trail, at the bottom of a hill. Turn right onto the main trail. A little later you will pass several side trails leading down to the reservoir. If you take one of these, retrace your steps after your exploration and continue on the main trail until you reach the bridge. Complete the circuit by crossing the bridge to your car.

Hike 4.9 Mineral Hill

> Easy 4-mile (one-way) wooded trail with numerous over-
> looks of Liberty Reservoir; recommended in all seasons.

Trail's Attractions

The Mineral Hill Trail parallels the southern shore of the Morgan Run area of the reservoir. It also runs almost parallel to Hike 4.2,

Winter stream scene along Mineral Hill Trail (Tom Herbert)

the Abandoned Mine–Coot Peninsula Trail, which follows the northern shore. The trail leads up and down gentle slopes, winding its way through a mature deciduous forest and a few pine plantations that are gradually being taken over by hardwoods.

An outstanding feature of the Mineral Hill Trail is its many impressive vistas of the reservoir. These views are especially nice in winter, when the trees are coated with ice and snow, or in autumn, when blazing colors extend from the trail down to the reservoir. Some of the scenes are enjoyable, however, even in the middle of summer.

This trail also offers many other attractions. In the summer, you will see a large area of wild roses in bloom near Pine Knob Road, and other wildflowers will enhance your visit in the spring. In addition, for those stalking foodstuffs, raspberries are plentiful along this trail. This is truly a trail for all seasons.

Directions

The western access to the trail is probably your best bet in poor weather conditions. It can be reached by following Liberty Road (Md. 26) approximately 12 miles west from Beltway Exit 18 to the intersection with Md. 32 in Eldersburg. Turn right and travel approximately 2.1 miles to the trail head on the right (.4 mile past Pine Knob Road). The trail runs up a hill and is marked by a No sign.

The eastern access is recommended in good weather. It can be reached by following Liberty Road approximately 8.7 miles from Beltway Exit 18 to Oakland Mills Road (the Oakland Mills Road intersection comes after you cross the first bridge over the reservoir on Liberty Road). Turn right onto Oakland Mills Road and proceed for approximately 1 mile to Oakland Road. Turn right onto Oakland Road and follow for .6 mile to Greenville Road, on the left. Follow Greenville Road to its terminus, where you will find the fire road.

When starting at the Greenville Road access, follow the fire road straight down the hill to the intersection. Turn left here, and you will be on the main trail. As you pass through a mature forest area and then through some pines that are gradually being replaced by

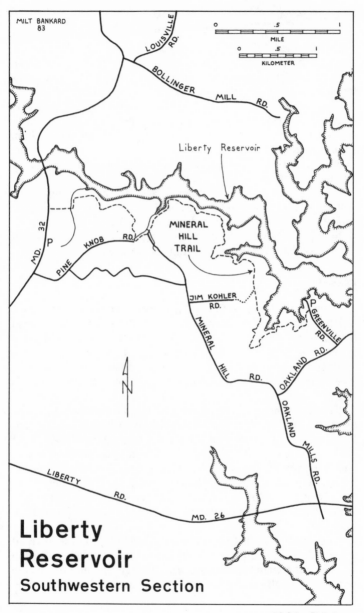

MILT BANKARD
83

LOUISVILLE RD.

BOLLINGER MILL RD.

Liberty Reservoir

MINERAL HILL TRAIL

MD. 32

P

PINE KNOB RD.

JIM KOHLER RD.

MINERAL HILL RD.

P GREENVILLE RD.

OAKLAND RD.

OAKLAND MILLS RD.

N

LIBERTY RD.

MD. 26

Liberty Reservoir
Southwestern Section

USGS Finksburg

hardwoods, you may notice some traffic noise in the distance. For the most part, however, the trail is fairly isolated.

When you reach the intersection with Pine Knob Road, turn right and follow Pine Knob Road for approximately .1 mile. Turn right onto the fire road (marked by fire road sign), next to a group of large pines. Follow this road all the way out to Md. 32 to cover the entire trail. To return, retrace your route.

Other accesses to the middle parts of the trail are available from Pine Knob Road, (reached from Md. 32), or from Jim Kohler Road. Jim Kohler Road is reached by turning onto Oakland Mills Road from Liberty Road, and traveling 2.2 miles to the intersection. Turn right onto Jim Kohler Road and follow it to its end.

5. Soldiers' Delight

Introduction to the Area

Soldiers' Delight, which is located in the western part of Baltimore County, was made a Natural Environmental Area in 1968. Operated by the Maryland Park Service, it is outstanding both for its great beauty and for its unique natural features. The area is admirably suited for hiking and nature study. Although its name is the subject of considerable curiosity and has been traced back to colonial times, no one is certain of its origin. It is said that soldiers in the service of King George III named the place Soldiers' Delight either because Indians could not surprise them as easily in the barren spaces as in the woods or because the local housewives baked cakes and pies for them. The area consists of serpentine rock barrens interspersed with forest. The barrens support only small trees: blackjack oak, post oak, and Virginia pine, while the forests contain both pines and hardwoods of several varieties. Deer Park Road, which runs mainly north and south through the middle of Soldiers' Delight, is customarily used as a dividing line between the east and west sides of the area. Ward's Chapel Road branches off from Deer Park Road in the northern part of Soldiers' Delight and runs to the southwest, intersecting Liberty Road about a mile east of the main bridge over Liberty Resevoir. A short distance west of Deer Park Road, two parallel electric power lines run north and south. Running along the power lines is a dirt road (restricted to use by maintenance vehicles of the Baltimore Gas and Electric Company and the park superintendent) that affords excellent walking for people who do not dislike steep grades. A part of the green and white trails (Hikes 5.1 and 5.2) lies along this dirt road.

There are many streams in Soldiers' Delight, most of them so small that they can be crossed with no difficulty. Those on the east side all feed Red Run, which in turn combines with Gwynns Falls on the McDonogh School property, southwest of Owings Mills. On the west side the two principal streams are Locust Run, toward the south, and Chimney Branch, toward the north. They meet west of

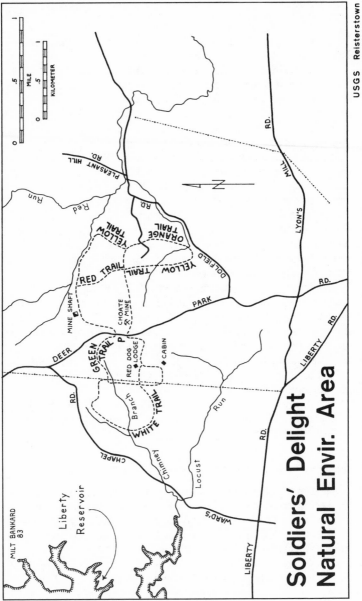

Soldiers' Delight
Natural Envir. Area

USGS Reisterstown

MILT BANKARD 83

Liberty Reservoir

45

Ward's Chapel Road and flow as one stream into Liberty Reservoir.

Geologically, Soldiers' Delight closely resembles Bare Hills, which lies just north of the Baltimore City line and is intersected by Falls Road and the Harrisburg Expressway (Interstate 83); however, Bare Hills has been so extensively developed that little of it is now in its natural condition (see Hike 10.2). The serpentine barrens in both areas contain chromite ore. Early in the nineteenth century, a company owned by Isaac Tyson began to work these deposits in order to obtain chromium for the manufacture of paint. The first working chromium mines in the world, they were abandoned when richer deposits were found in several foreign countries. During the First World War they were reopened briefly to provide chromium for the manufacture of steel, but since then they have remained unused. Many of the mines are partly filled with fallen rock and trash. Some are vertical shafts; others are sloping tunnels. Do not attempt to enter any of them.

The peculiar geological character of Soldiers' Delight has led to a special type of vegetation, including many varieties of wildflowers, some of which are generally very rare. You may not pick flowers or dig up plants in Soldiers' Delight. Off-road vehicles are also forbidden as is the use of firearms or other weapons. Although trash cans are provided in some places, littering is a problem. We encourage hikers not only to refrain from littering themselves but also to remove litter left by others.

Poison ivy is abundant in parts of Soldiers' Delight, though its presence should not discourage any careful hiker. For precautions against it see chapter 3.

Access to the Soldiers' Delight Area

All formally designated walks in Soldiers' Delight begin from the scenic overlook on Deer Park Road. It can most easily be reached from Baltimore by following Liberty Road (Md. 26) west from Beltway Exit 18 for 3 miles to the traffic light at McDonogh Road (Maryland National Bank is on the right across McDonogh Road). Continue on Liberty Road 1.9 miles, to Deer Park Road; a large elevated pale green tank here is a useful landmark. Turn right onto Deer Park Road and drive north for 2.3 miles, to the overlook. This can scarcely be missed; it has a Maryland Park Service sign and a Baltimore County Historical Society sign, both on the left, and parking space for all but the largest hiking group. The elevation is high, nearly seven hundred feet above sea level, and there is an exceptionally fine view over Carroll County to the west. Although it is not visible from the overlook, Liberty Reservoir is situated in the hollow a short distance to the west. The western side of the Soldiers' Delight Natural Environmental Area is contiguous with the Liberty Reservoir watershed area, making it possible for hikers to pass from one area to the other without trespassing on private land. This part of Soldiers' Delight, however, does not contain designated trails (see Hike 4.5 and 4.6).

The Deer Park Road overlook can also be reached by following Reisterstown Road (Md. 140) 1.2 miles northwest from the Beltway, to the second traffic light. Turn left on McDonogh Road and follow it to Lyons Mill Road, passing an American Legion post on your left. Turn left (west) on Lyons Mill Road, continue to Deer Park Road, and turn right (north). You can also follow Painters Mill Road from Owings Mills, turn right onto South Dolfield Road, left onto Dolfield Road, and finally, right onto Deer Park Road. A third route from Reisterstown Road is to follow Berrymans' Lane southwestward to Deer Park Road, then turn left, and continue south to the overlook.

At the south end of the parking area at the overlook is a sign with pointers in five colors: green, white, yellow, orange, and red. The green and white trails lie on the west side; the other three lie on the east and are partly coextensive. Use caution when crossing Deer Park Road, especially with children, because traffic moves quickly.

Getting Lost

If you are unfamiliar with Soldiers' Delight, it is easy to get lost in the woods, although somewhat more difficult in the barrens, where it is possible to see for a greater distance. If you are on the east side and can hear traffic noises, they are most likely to be from Deer Park Road. The only other possibility is Dolfield Road, which you may hear from the south end of the loop that forms a part of both the yellow (counterclockwise) and the orange trails (clockwise). If you are on the west side, the high towers of the two parallel power lines will frequently be visible and will help you orient yourself. Traffic noises on this side will be from Deer Park Road, which is located to the east of the power line, or from Ward's Chapel Road, most of which lies to the west of the power line and follows a northeast-southwest direction. It is also well to remember that the general slope of the land on the west side is downward from the overlook and from Red Dog Lodge. A compass will be useful if you feel in danger of getting lost.

Hike 5.1 Red Dog Lodge, Cabin, and Power Line

Green trail: 2-mile circuit hike, mostly in the open; scenic; several unusual species of wildflower in spring and fall; some steep grades.

The green trail runs southward through the woods, almost parallel to the road, then comes out into the open and joins the road to Red Dog Lodge. Built as a hunting lodge in 1912 by the Dolfield family, the lodge is kept closed, but there are picnic tables and a trash can at its north side and sanitary facilities to the south. To the west there is an extensive view into Carroll County. The trail winds toward the left on the near side of the building and continues southward out into the open past a small two-story log cabin, said to have been an office of the mining company in the early nineteenth century. The trail continues to the northwest corner of a patch of woods located south of the cabin; here there is a signpost with a green pointer and the number 23. Bear right and walk north along the power-line clearing to signpost 24, which is situated on high ground from which Red Dog Lodge is visible on the right (east). Still in the powerline clearing, continue down the hill to the north until you reach the stream. There are two signposts on the far side of the stream, on opposite sides of the clearing. Neither is numbered, but both have green arrows pointing to the right (east). Follow the trail up the stream bed. It finally separates from the stream on the north side, continues up the hill, and reaches Deer Park Road immediately north of the overlook.

Hike 5.2 Red Dog Lodge, Cabin, Power Line, and Barrens

White trail: 3-mile circuit hike, partly in the barrens, partly in the woods; some excellent views; some steep grades.

This trail is the same as the green trail until you reach the point where the power line crosses the stream and the green trail goes off to the right toward the overlook. From this stream crossing continue north along the power line to the first white pointer, turn left and walk westward across the barrens, carefully following the white pointers. (The signposts after number 24 do not show numbers.) The trail continues in a counterclockwise direction, crosses a stream, and ascends through the barrens. It then will enter the woods, cross the power line just west of Red Dog Lodge, continue to Red Dog Lodge, and return to the overlook on the same trail used to begin the hike.

Hike 5.3 Choate Mine and Forest, I

Yellow trail: 3-mile circuit hike, mostly in the woods but with some stretches through the barrens; good views in the barrens section; mostly level but with some gentle grades; good for those interested in wildflowers or birding.

Pick up this trail opposite the overlook and slightly to the south. In this area, the yellow, orange, and red trails all follow the same path. Because directions for all three trails are given on each signpost, it is advisable to check both sides of each one to avoid missing a turn. Continue until you reach the Choate Mine, which is not more than a five-minute walk from the overlook and has its own marker. Because the mouth of the mine opens toward the east, you are likely not to see it until you are almost past it. A short distance from the mine on your right (southeast) is a stone foundation, the only remnant of a building formerly used in the processing of chromium ore. It is overgrown and badly infested with poison ivy. The trail continues beyond the mine in an easterly direction. It is likely to be muddy after rain, so you may have to walk on the slightly higher ground on either side of the trail.

At the intersection of two trails, there are two signposts a short distance apart, one bearing the number 4. Here the three trails separate: yellow goes right (south), orange straight ahead (east), and red left (north). Turn right on the yellow trail. After an easy, nearly level fifteen-minute walk through pine woods, you will arrive at a signpost with a yellow pointer but no number. Near it, on the left, are several old mine holes. About five minutes' walk south of the mine holes, you will see signpost 6; you are now very close to Dolfield Road. Bear left (eastward) over the barrens, then northward back into the woods to signpost 7. Just beyond it, on the left, is a small pond. Continue north through the woods to signpost 8. A gravel road intersects the trail here. It leads northwestward to a private residence and eastward toward Dolfield Road. Cross the gravel road and follow the trail through a cleared strip in the field, past signposts 9 and 10 and back into the woods. Signposts 8, 9, 10, and 11 follow in close succession. After this, the trail becomes somewhat confused and requires close attention. A barnlike building should be visible on the right, a short distance away from the intersection of a wider trail. The trail continues in a northerly direction, leading mostly downhill through the woods. Mountain laurel is abundant here and usually blooms at the end of May or in early June.

Soon after passing signpost 14, you will see a small swampy area on your right. Continue downhill past signpost 15; there will be a small stream on your right. At the bottom of the hill you will meet a more prominent trail, with a larger stream immediately beyond it. Turn left and you will see signpost 16 on your right. Continue along this trail in an upstream direction. After about ten minutes you will leave the stream, enter the barrens, go over a small hill, and reach a signpost with yellow, orange, and red pointers but with no number shown. After this, the trail continues toward the west. At one point, you will see on your right a metal fence that surrounds a vertical mine shaft; it is possible to lean on the fence and see down into the mine. From here the trail continues, turning once to the left and once to the right, and soon reaches Deer Park Road just north of the overlook.

Hike 5.4 Choate Mine and Forest, II

Orange trail: 2-mile circuit hike, mostly in the woods; almost all level.

Proceed from the overlook exactly as for Hike 5.3, past the Choate Mine to signpost 4. From here the orange trail continues straight ahead to signpost 12. After this, it follows the same path as the yellow trail, but in the reverse direction (orange travels clockwise, yellow counterclockwise). You will pass signposts 11, 10, 9, 8, 7, 6, and, after about twenty minutes, return to signpost 4. From here, you can either turn left and go back past the Choate Mine to the overlook or continue straight ahead (north), following the markers for the red trail. When you reach the unnumbered signpost that followed signpost 16 in the description of the yellow trail, follow the directions for the yellow trail back to the overlook.

Hike 5.5 Choate Mine, Forest, and Barrens

Red trail: 1-mile circuit hike, the shortest of the four hikes; almost all level; affords a view of a vertical mine shaft inside a metal fence.

Proceed from the overlook past the Choate Mine to signpost 4, exactly as in Hikes 5.3 and 5.4. Turn left and continue through the woods and into the barrens. A walk of about three minutes will take you to signpost 5. Bear right (east), and in about ten minutes you will reach the unnumbered signpost described near the end of the account of Hike 5.3 (yellow trail). Return to the overlook using the same route as described for the yellow and orange trails.

6. Prettyboy Reservoir

Introduction to the Area

Prettyboy area hikes have an unusual character. The terrain surrounding Prettyboy Reservoir provides some of the more challenging hiking in the Baltimore area. The rocky substratum is composed of undivided Wissahickon schist, a western piedmont metasedimentary rock. It has weathered, giving the area steeper gorges and more exposed rock than any of the other hiking areas near Baltimore.

The region has an early nineteenth-century flavor. Now, as in the early 1800s, it consists mostly of farms and very small towns. You will discern many vestiges of the early settlers' habitation: old stone and log-and-mortar cabins, fieldstone fences, abandoned mill dams, and weathered churches and graveyards.

Prettyboy Reservoir, formed in 1936 by the damming of the Gunpowder Falls, is a Baltimore City reservoir. A small creek near the dam, named many years ago for a little girl's favorite pony, gives the reservoir its name. The reservoir and the 5,880 acres of planted pines and natural deciduous woodlands around it are maintained by the Baltimore City Bureau of Engineering, Water Division. The bureau maintains an extensive system of fire and maintenance roads, some of which make fine hiking trails.

Prettyboy Reservoir is maintained so as to keep Loch Raven Reservoir, downstream on the Gunpowder Falls, filled to a fairly constant depth. Since Loch Raven Reservoir requires different amounts of water from Prettyboy Reservoir in different seasons, and since the shores of Prettyboy Reservoir are steep, a permanent vegetation is unable to establish itself; thus, the shoreline is somewhat unsightly. It is probably better, however, to keep the system as it is now, letting Prettyboy Reservoir fluctuate and Loch Raven Reservoir remain stable, than to have the ecological and scenic values of both dependent on the city's water needs.

Those who hike the Prettyboy Reservoir watershed trails should realize that they are enjoying a privilege that can be revoked. They

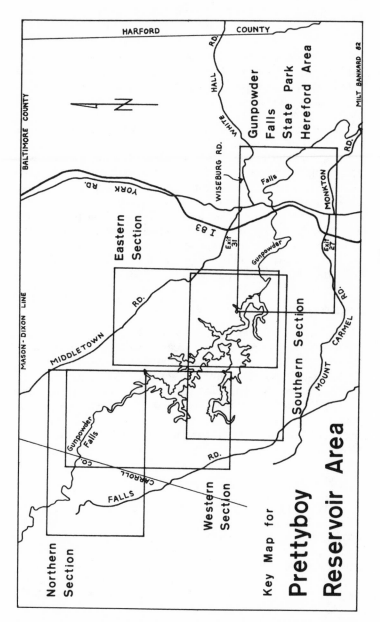

Key Map for
Prettyboy Reservoir Area

Gunpowder Falls State Park Hereford Area

Eastern Section

Southern Section

Northern Section

Western Section

HARFORD COUNTY

BALTIMORE COUNTY

MASON - DIXON LINE

YORK RD.

HALL RD.

WHITE HALL

WISEBURG RD.

MONKTON

Exit 31

Exit 27

I 83

Falls

Gunpowder

MIDDLETOWN RD.

MOUNT CARMEL RD.

CO.

CARROLL

Gunpowder Falls

FALLS RD.

MILT BANKARD 82

should, therefore, have a heightened sense of responsibility about the land, waters, and wildlife. The same courtesies hikers should always observe are especially important here: they should leave no sign of their passing—take no blooms, cut no branches, and strew no lunch debris.

The watershed lands of Prettyboy Reservoir and the other two city reservoirs comprise Baltimore's greatest natural unspoiled areas. Their value as scenic, educational, and hiking resources will become more apparent in years to come. The bureau's land protection policies have been threatened in the past and will be again, unless the public gives its support. The bureau now operates with no support for this unofficial part of its program—the preservation of wildlands—and with very limited funds for supervision, patrol, and enforcement of its regulations for recreational use.

See chapter 1 for information about citizen involvement in supporting the bureau's policies.

Regulations

The Bureau of Engineering has several regulations that must be observed if the public is to retain access to these lands. Pollution of the waters of the reservoirs or their tributaries is prohibited. Use the sanitary facilities that are provided near the fishing and picnicking areas. You are not permitted to skate, build fires, park or drive vehicles (including motorcycles) except on surfaced roads, swim, wade, or use firearms. Boating is allowed only by permit. Fishing licenses are required. No camping is permitted Never park a car so as to block a fire road.

Access to the Prettyboy Area

Though the Prettyboy Reservoir area is a considerable distance north of Baltimore, I 83 (the Harrisburg Expressway) cuts the driving time to about an hour.

Except for the Civilian Conservation Corps (CCC) Trail, which is reached from Exit 27 (Mount Carmel and Hereford roads), all hikes listed here use Exit 31 (Middletown Road), about 16 miles north of the Beltway. Middletown Road runs northwest from I 83.

Intersecting with it on the left are the roads leading to the starting points of all the hikes except the CCC Trail. Rayville Road leads to the Spook Hill Trail, Parsonage Road to the Frog Hollow Trail, and Beckleysville Road to the five remaining trails. You will see old Middletown and Gunpowder churches just before you reach the Beckleysville Road intersection.

Getting Lost

Getting lost on a watershed trail should not be easy; however, if you do get lost, you should have little difficulty reorienting yourself. The watershed boundaries are usually marked—by landowners' barbed-wire fences, frequent small round metal bureau markers on trees, or occasional yellow or white signs. All markers face away from watershed property. Because the trails rim a valley, farms, homes, or roads are always nearby on the uphill side. Make use of the maps along with the trail descriptions.

Hike 6.1 Spook Hill

Easy 2-mile (round-trip) wooded walk, leading to a rocky point with views of the reservoir.

Trail's Attractions

Spook Hill, given its name because of the weird tree-groves and loud croaking in nearby Frog Hollow, is a secluded, wooded area that was occupied by members of the Mathews family for several generations. The trail leads through pines and deciduous woods to House Rock, a point that has a fine view and is a delightful place to picnic. Underwater at the point is a rock overhang that once sheltered Indians, hence the name House Rock. In winter the adventurous hiker may bushwhack from House Rock northwards, through the trees along the shore to sheer rugged cliffs for some glorious views of the reservoir. If you bushwhack near the shore of Frog Hollow Cove, you may see the old embankment of a railroad (never completed) that was to connect the Northern Central Railroad with the Hanover branch of the Western Maryland Railroad.

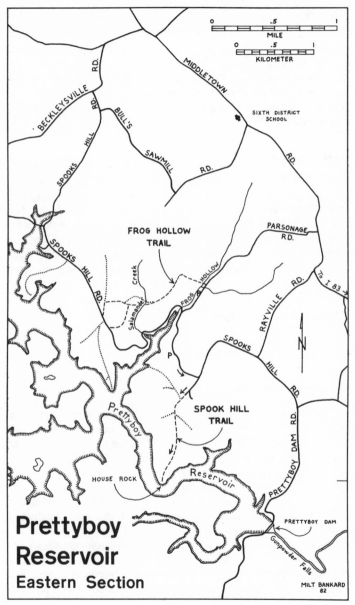

Prettyboy
Reservoir
Eastern Section

SIXTH DISTRICT
SCHOOL

FROG HOLLOW
TRAIL

PARSONAGE
R.D.

SPOOK HILL
TRAIL

HOUSE ROCK

PRETTYBOY DAM

Gunpowder Falls

MILT BANKARD
82

Hereford   USGS   New Freedom

56

Trail Directions

To reach Spook Hill take Middletown Road northwest for approximately 2 miles from I 83 to Rayville Road and turn left onto Rayville Road. Turn right at the next intersection, onto Spooks Hill Road. After half a mile, watch for a gravel road at a right angle bend. This is the trail entrance. Rather than park along the narrow shoulder, drive further to the overlook, park there, and walk back.

You can reach the fire-road trail by walking straight ahead on the gravel road, past the houses. (There is a No Trespassing sign here, but it does not apply to the Bureau's land, which is along the right side of the road.) When the road turns to the left, keep walking straight ahead onto the fire road (the gravel road is private beyond this point). Follow a new bulldozed fire road that curves slightly to the left. (The old fire road leads to a dead end at Frog Hollow Cove and, at present, is blocked by many fallen trees.) At an open area the fire road bears to the right toward House Rock. Walk along the ridge, avoiding side logging roads. At the end of the fire road, a small trail leads straight ahead to the rocky point.

Return via the same route.

Hike 6.2 Frog Hollow

Moderate, mostly wooded, delightful 2-mile (one-way) trail; recommended in all seasons.

Trail's Attractions

Frog Hollow Trail is one of the most delightful trails in the Prettyboy Reservoir area. Frog Hollow was given its name because of the myriad of frogs that inhabit the small valley, or hollow, surrounding the stream of the same name. The hollow is marshy and its clear-running stream is lined with ferns and wildflowers. In the spring, the area is filled with the sounds of birds, as well as frogs. Sit quietly and you may see a red fox pass by.

The hilly trail travels through mostly deciduous woods sprinkled with wild azalea, mountain laurel, and dogwood. It crosses streams in several places. The observant hiker will notice wildflowers such as bloodroot, rue anemone, arbutus, and toothwort. Please leave them for others to enjoy.

Trail Directions

To reach Frog Hollow, follow Middletown Road northwest approximately 2.5 miles from I 83, until Parsonage Road enters on the left. Turn onto Parsonage Road and drive 1.1 miles, to an overgrown field on your left; there you will see a small county maintenance sign. Park along the wide shoulder. The trail entrance is on your right. Frog Hollow trail begins with a stream crossing and a steep ascent out of the hollow. It continues up and over the ridge, crosses a stream and climbs again, then is fairly level until it drops abruptly, running down to Salamander Creek. The trail on your right at the creek leads upstream, through a privately owned wood lot. The trail bearing to the left leads uphill and joins the right-hand trail, near boundary marker 66. Bear left, continuing on the fire road along the ridge to an intersection with a dirt road. Turn left onto this road. When you reach Spooks Hill Road, cross it and pick up the fire road again, almost directly across the road. Take the left-hand fork and continue to the turn-around area. From here, you can go straight ahead on a narrow trail, to a point with a view of the reservoir and Frog Hollow Cove, or you can go down a steep trail on the right, to some rocks that jut into the water—a lovely picnic spot. Please leave no trash.

Return to Spooks Hill Road. Cross the road and walk to your right along the shoulder a short distance, until you see a fire road entrance on your left. Turn left and follow this fire road, making a loop back to Salamander Creek. From the creek, retrace your steps to Parsonage Road.

This hike may easily be combined with the Spook Hill Trail.

Hike 6.3 Gunpowder Loop

Easy 4.5-mile partial circuit along river, wooded ridge, and farm fields; recommended in all seasons.

Trail's Attractions

The Gunpowder Loop is an easy hike; mostly level, it is cool and shady in summer. The trail follows the ridge above the Gunpowder Falls Valley and loops back along the river. A variety of habitats is represented: rocky and fern-bedecked streams, open cornfields and

Prettyboy Dam (Courtesy of the Baltimore County Chamber of Commerce)

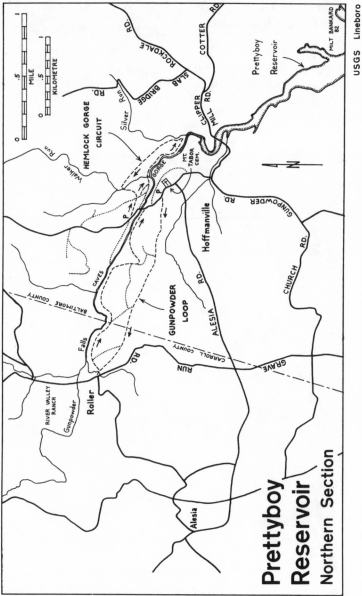

Prettyboy Reservoir
Northern Section

HEMLOCK GORGE CIRCUIT

GUNPOWDER LOOP

Silver Run

Walker Run

GORGE

MT. TABOR CEM.

Hoffmanville

CAVES

Falls

Roller

Alesia

River Valley Ranch

Gunpowder

BALTIMORE COUNTY

CARROLL COUNTY

RUN

ALESIA RD.

CHURCH RD.

GUNPOWDER RD.

CLIPPER MILL RD.

SLAB BRIDGE RD.

ROCKDALE RD.

COTTER RD.

GRAVE

Prettyboy Reservoir

MILT BANKARD 82

N

USGS   Lineboro

MILE

.5

KILOMETRE

.5

0

pastures, deciduous woods, some beautiful hemlocks, and exposed rock formations.

The town of Hoffmanville, near the trail entrance, was named for the man who established a paper mill here in the 1770s and who later supplied paper for money printed by the Continental Congress. Remnants of the old Hoffman ice dam can be seen near the bridge on Gunpowder Road, opposite the entrance to Hemlock Gorge Circuit.

The town of Roller is located at the western end of the trail, at Grave Run Road. Owned by River Valley Ranch, the town features bison in the pasture, a stagecoach, horseback riding, and refreshments in season.

On the northeast bank of Gunpowder Falls is the bed of a long-abandoned railroad, wet underfoot and partly overgrown. At the trail's end, near Bettys Run, are some small caves. Ferns and wildflowers abound nearby. Bettys Run is typical of streams of this area. As it tumbles over the exposed rock of the gorge, sunlight reflects its ripples on the rock. In autumn, you can glimpse the bright red of the low-growing partridge berry along its banks. All the common stream and valley birds are represented here, and the quiet hiker may encounter a pair of nesting wood ducks.

Directions

Follow the directions for Hike 6.5. At the intersection of Gunpowder and Clipper Mill roads, follow Gunpowder Road to the right .3 mile to the graveyard at Hoffmanville. Park on the shoulder just beyond the graveyard and walk along the road to the gravel fire road entrance on your left.

Begin the Gunpowder Loop here. For most of its length, the trail is a grass-covered or leaf-strewn dirt fire road. It leads first through a pine plantation and then along the edge of the bureau lands; planted pines will be on your right and cornfields and pastures on your left. The trail passes through a small wood patch and soon ascends a steep hill to the deciduous forest on the ridge. Along the ridge, old dead-end logging spurs lead off the main trail, which may be confusing. Keep in mind that the main fire road keeps to the spine of the ridge, even as it makes a gradual descent to Grave Run Road.

Near Grave Run Road, the trail traverses privately owned land. Gunpowder Loop has been used by the public for years, however, and the owners permit hikers to walk through the area on their good behavior. When you reach Grave Run Road you will see River Valley Ranch to your right. To continue the hike, take the footpath at the edge of the pasture immediately to your right. This will lead you down to Gunpowder Falls. At the river, follow the trail along an unused fire road (passing the fire-road cut-off leading to the ridge). You will probably have trouble following the trail, which almost disappears. Just keep near the river—the ground becomes uneven and difficult to walk on—and you will see the trail again. It leads up to the ridge (avoid right-hand trails) and loops left back down to the river.

You may want to visit adjacent Hemlock Gorge. If you do, allow plenty of time for thorough enjoyment.

Hike 6.4 Hemlock Gorge Circuit

Two-mile (round-trip) walk to secluded glen in scenic, historic area; rough trail.

Trail's Attractions

Hemlock Gorge is unique in the Baltimore area. A short walk from the road leads you to this almost completely unspoiled spot, where huge old hemlocks shade a steep-sided valley. The gorge is strewn with large boulders and filled with the sound of cascading water. You will see ferns and wildflowers of many kinds; birds abound in the gorge. You can spend a rewarding summer's day in this area, identifying and enjoying the wildlife with the help of a fern, bird, or wildflower book.

Directions

This hike starts .4 mile beyond the Gunpowder Loop entrance on Gunpowder Road. Cross the bridge over Gunpowder Falls beyond Hoffmanville. There is adequate space for several cars to park on the wide shoulder beyond the bridge.

To traverse the circuit walk uphill on the old fire road on your right, above Gunpowder Falls. At the top of the hill, leave the fire road, turn right, and head downhill to the river. Cross Walker Run and continue through the gorge to Silver Run. Beyond the rocky gorge, the floodplain area is overgrown with spiny vines (perfoliate tearthumb); it may be difficult to walk through in midsummer. Circle the base of the ridge at Silver Run and return to the fire road. Follow it back to the car.

Hike 6.5 Laurel Highlands

Strenuous, continuously hilly trail, 5.5 miles one way, with varied wildlife habitats; shorter, easier hikes possible; recommended in spring, summer, and autumn.

Trail's Attractions

The Laurel Highlands area is mostly wooded, with occasional open spots. Adjacent to the bureau's boundary line are grazing pastures and meadows of wildflowers. Mountain laurel is pretty in June, and you may see a great variety of birds, as well as the seasonal succession of wildflowers. In springtime, carp breed in the marsh at the mouth of Grave Run; you can see them stirring up the water close to shore. The marsh is also a good place for water birds. The site of the old Rockdale paper mill is submerged nearby.

Laurel Highlands Trail offers varied scenery in a hilly terrain. The most interesting sections are the middle and the north end. Prettyboy Reservoir is only occasionally visible from the trail.

Only experienced hikers should undertake the full-length trail, especially the round trip. During partial thaws in late winter and in wet early spring weather, the trail will be slippery and, therefore, as tiring as a ten-mile hike. Nature watchers likely to tarry along the way and families with young children should try shorter portions of the trail.

Directions

Follow Middletown Road northwest approximately 4.5 miles from I 83, to the intersection with Beckleysville Road. Turn left and drive a short distance, to Cotter Road, which forks to the right.

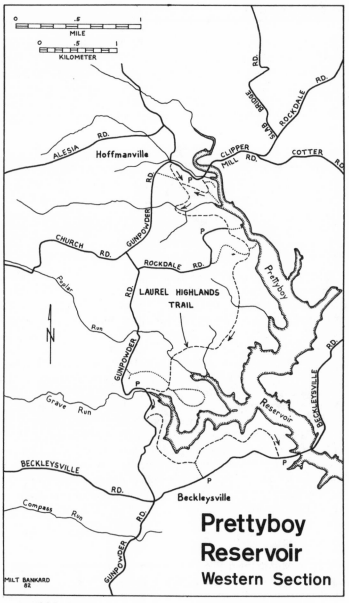

Prettyboy
Reservoir
Western Section

MILT BANKARD
82

USGS Lineboro

After 2 miles, Cotter Road intersects with Clipper Mill Road. Turn left onto Clipper Mill Road and follow it .7 mile, crossing a bridge, to the intersection with Gunpowder Road. Park on Clipper Mill Road.

The trail starts at this intersection. Although it is unmarked, the entrance is easy to spot. The wide path ascends the steep, laurel-covered hillside and is not difficult to follow. Rockdale Road and the path join for a few yards at one point. Past Rockdale Road, you may want to explore the short spur trail on the right; it passes through an older forest, entirely different from the rest of the trail.

The end of Rockdale Road is a good alternate access point for those wanting a shorter hike; two additional entrances are available near the bridge over Grave Run on Gunpowder Road. To reach any of these, turn left onto Gunpowder Road from Clipper Mill Road.

When starting on Rockdale Road, it is best to park (two cars only) near the end of the hard road, at the sharp bend, avoiding private property. The end of Rockdale Road is blocked and no parking is permitted. The trail begins on the fire road just beyond the gate blocking the road. The entrance south of Grave Run, on Gunpowder Road, is a distance up the hill, on the left, at an old blocked-off macadam road. The trail on the north side of Grave Run is a dirt fire road, easy to spot.

Beyond Rockdale Road the trail descends, crosses Grave Run, and continues to Beckleysville Road.

For one-way hikes a car at the south trail entrance, .3 mile west of the Beckleysville Road bridge, is necessary. There is adequate parking on the shoulders near the bridge.

Hike 6.6 Shamberger's Peninsula

Easy, wooded 2-mile (one-way) walk in isolated area; recommended in all seasons except hunting season.

Trail's Attractions

Shamberger's Peninsula Trail follows a level, grass-covered old roadbed to an isolated area. Off the peninsula's tip is the site of the old Shamberger grist mill, owned and operated by a family that, in 1790, established one of the first farms in the region. Family groups and others desiring a pleasant, easy stroll should enjoy this hike.

The trail passes through largely deciduous woodland, cool and shady in summer. The pines near the trail entrance offer good winter protection for deer. Near the tip of the peninsula, the trail crosses a narrow neck of land with water on both sides. Watch for water birds here.

About a mile from the entrance, a side trail on the right leads to a small rocky promontory, which is a good vantage point, a fine picnic site, or a fishing spot. You will see Virginia (or scrub) pines and pitch pines on your right; deciduous woods will be on your left. Mountain laurel covers the distant hillside. Pennsylvania mound-building ants have made large anthills along the trail. Farther along, a fire road on the left leads to an area where the Beckleysville Bridge is visible in winter.

Avoid the whole area in deer-hunting season.

Directions

To reach Shamberger's Peninsula Trail follow Middletown Road northwest to Beckleysville Road, approximately 4.5 miles from Exit 31 on I 83. Follow Beckleysville Road roughly 3.2 miles, over the bridge and up the hill to the trail entrance, which is marked by a white Bureau of Engineering sign. Near the entrance there is space to park on the road shoulder. Do not block the entrance to the fire road with parked cars.

The trail is easy to follow all the way. Add about half a mile to the total mileage for each side trail.

Hike 6.7 Prettyboy Trail

Long (about 10.5 miles one way) but mostly level wooded walk, with many views of the reservoir; several access points can be used to divide the hike into shorter walks.

Trail's Attractions

Along most of its length, this trail follows the shoreline of the reservoir, thereby affording more water views than other trails in

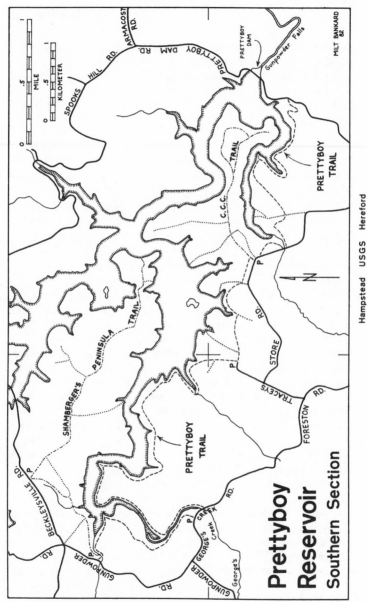

Prettyboy Reservoir
Southern Section

Lineboro USGS New Freedom

Hampstead USGS Hereford

MILT BANKARD 82

the Prettyboy Reservoir area. It traverses both deciduous and pine woods; the pine woods near the intersection of the CCC Trail and Prettyboy Trail are particularly beautiful—tall and straight and are surrounded by almost no undergrowth. Yellow, white, and purple violets, as well as spring-beauties, wild lilies of the valley, and other wildflowers, abound.

Directions

Follow the directions to Shamberger's Peninsula Trail and park in the same spot; both trails start nearby.

Take the right-hand fire road through the pines on the south side of the road. The trail leaves this fire road at the right side of the first big bend. Follow the blue markers. (On the far side of a stream crossing, a side trail comes in on your right. This leads to Gunpowder Road, where there is parking for two cars.) The trail continues along the shore, crosses a slight ridge, and leads to George's Creek Road, where there is a good parking spot. Cross George's Creek on the highway bridge. The trail continues just beyond the bridge, eventually crossing an overgrown road. An extension of Foreston Road, this road leads to private land. Continue along the shore trail. Well-worn side trails intersect with the main path in several places, so keep your eyes open and stay on the blue-marked trail. It leads up to the hard-surfaced road (an extension of Tracey Store Road), where there is parking space. Turn left (crossing a cable) and walk down an old road, past an old house site. Follow the blue markers on the trail that leads to the CCC Trail (see map). Turn right, toward the large parking space. Walk along the highway's left shoulder to the trail entrance. Hidden in the pines, the entrance is about half the distance from the parking area to a small concrete culvert. The trail loops through the pines back to the highway.

Cross the highway bridge and find the trail close to the stream on the far side. Again, follow the blue markers through beautiful pines (avoid two well-worn, unmarked trails—one on your right and one straight ahead). You will cross an old road after entering deciduous woods. Continue straight on another old road. Blue markers are farther apart here, as the route is obvious. The trail becomes rocky underfoot and may be slippery in wet weather. It leads to Prettyboy Dam Road.

No parking is permitted near Prettyboy Dam on Saturdays, Sundays, or holidays; parking is allowed for only twenty minutes on weekdays. Therefore, this may be an access point on weekends or holidays only if you park a considerable distance from the dam area. A round-trip hike, from Tracey Store Road to the dam and back, for example, may be a better choice.

You can also plan one-way hikes with car shuttles between any of the access points mentioned above.

Hike 6.8 CCC Trail

Easy 2-mile (round-trip) woodland walk on excellent trail.

Trail's Attractions

The CCC Trail is so named because it was installed by the Civilian Conservation Corps in the 1930s, when Prettyboy Dam was built. It is a fine hike for those wanting a quiet, easy stroll through the woods. The trail is covered with grass and, in some places, pine needles. Common spring and summer wildflowers grow along the path. It is gently sloping, wide, and clear in all places.

The CCC Trail winds through dense pine plantations, where you may see deer, to an old house site. Then it leads to the rocky end of the peninsula, where there is an open, relatively young deciduous forest, which includes scattered mountain laurels and dogwoods; along the loop, you may also see table-mountain pines. The rocky, acid soil of the peninsula supports plants such as spotted wintergreen (identifiable the year round—use your pocket reference books) and many ferns. In the winter, there are good views of the water from the loop trail. The spur that leads to the water's edge is the bed of a long-abandoned road.

Trail Directions

To reach the CCC Trail take Mount Carmel Road (Exit 27) west to Evna Road, 1.7 miles from I 83. Turn right onto Evna Road—a delightful, twisting old road—and follow it (roughly 1.3 miles) to the intersection with Falls Road (not to be confused with Md. 25, also called Falls Road). Turn left and follow it a short distance to where it feeds into Prettyboy Dam Road. Continue in the same direction on Prettyboy Dam Road for a short distance, until you reach Tracey Store Road. Finally, turn right onto Tracey Store Road. The entrance to the CCC Trail is near the second bend in the road, at the second Bureau of Engineering sign. Park cars in the wide areas.

The trails are very easy to follow. When hiking the CCC Trail, if time is available, you may want to explore the old road that leads to the water rather than the fire road spur.

7. Hereford Area of the Gunpowder Falls State Park

Introduction to the Area

The Gunpowder Falls is a river that runs some 40 miles diagonally across Baltimore County, mostly on public land, passing through Prettyboy and Loch Raven reservoirs. Another river, the Little Gunpowder Falls, forms most of the boundary between Baltimore and Harford counties. These rivers join each other shortly before emptying into an arm of the Chesapeake Bay called the Gunpowder River. The Gunpowder Falls State Park, with an area of about 11,000 acres, is scattered along all three of these rivers. The Hereford Area of the Gunpowder Falls State Park contains over 3,000 acres, extending along the Gunpowder Falls from Big Falls Road, east of the town of Hereford, to Baltimore City Watershed Property at Prettyboy Reservoir. It is readily reached from I 83, via Exit 27 (Mount Carmel Road) or Exit 31 (Middletown Road) (see map).

The Hereford Area of the park is a most attractive hiking area, with many miles of well-marked trails plus endless opportunities for off-path roaming, through the forests and along some of the side streams. The terrain ranges from open fields and gentle wooded slopes at the higher levels to precipitous ledges bordering the depths of the Gunpowder Falls Valley. The river itself varies from placid to turbulent. Along its shores and those of its tributaries flowers abound in season. In a day's birding, you may see Carolina chickadees, titmice, an indigo bunting, cardinals, a cuckoo, phoebes, peewees, vultures, an occasional hawk, a kingfisher, various woodpeckers, and several species of warbler, including worm-eating, yellow, yellowthroat, prairie, parula, and the Louisiana waterthrush. You may also see an occasional deer and, rarely, a fox. Evidence of beaver is abundant along the river, and beaver themselves have been seen toward dusk. Historical features in the area include many abandoned roads, old foundations, and, along Panther Branch, the remnants of earth dams and water-wheel pits.

All park users should respect park regulations, which include the following: no littering; no fires, except in fireplaces provided at

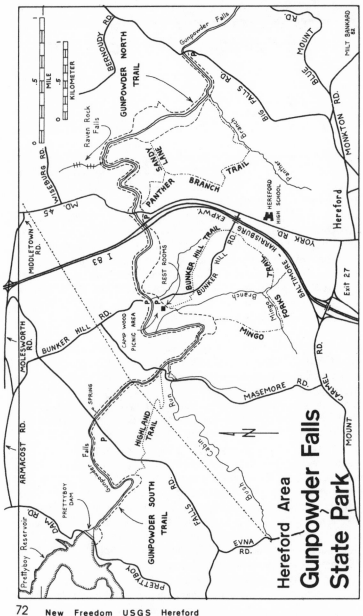

Hereford Area
**Gunpowder Falls
State Park**

the Bunker Hill picnic area (Camp Wood); no alcoholic beverages; no camping, except by special permission, which is sometimes granted to organized youth groups for camping at Bunker Hill Road; and no motorized vehicles off the highways. For information, contact the Gunpowder Falls State Park Headquarters, (301) 592-2897.

A new development plan for the park, approved in 1981, will probably result in some changes in the Hereford area over the next few years, including relocation of parking lots and minor displacements of hiking trails. These changes should cause no problems for hikers, however, since the trails are well marked.

At present, sanitary facilities and reliable drinking water are provided only at the Camp Wood picnic area, at the foot of Bunker Hill Road on the south side of the river (reached from York Road), from late spring to early fall.

Parcels of private land remain within the park boundaries, but owners do not generally object to the passage of well-behaved hikers who leave no rubbish and do not approach the houses.

Hiking trails totaling nearly 20 miles were developed in the Hereford area from 1970 to 1972 under the auspices of the Greater Baltimore Group of the Sierra Club, with the permission and encouragement of the park authorities. Since 1976 the Mountain Club of Maryland has assisted park personnel in maintaining these trails. All of them have been marked with colored disks and occasional signs. Some of the trails are also used by horseback riders; additional riding trails are planned for the near future. Hikers should be alert for signs and other trail markers, so that they do not turn mistakenly onto the riding trails or other unmarked tracks.

Please help keep the trails free of litter by carrying out your own rubbish and at least a little of what less thoughtful individuals have left.

Parking for most of the trails is available where the access roads, shown on the accompanying map, approach the river. It is absolutely essential not to obstruct any service road when you park, because immediate access may be needed in emergencies. As of 1982, no parking suitable for hikers is permitted at Prettyboy Dam. Parking on Falls Road near the river is limited to a small lot about .1 mile southwest of the bridge. A few cars may also be parked beside the road at the intersection of the Highland Trail and Falls Road, but they must not block the entrance to the fire road. Organized groups with many cars may seek advance permission to park at Hereford High School (301– 472–2341 or 301–329–6216).

Various trails are described below, along with some instructions to help you find them, in case signs or markers have been disturbed. Directions for several suggested circuit hikes follow the trail descriptions.

Bunker Hill Trail

This short, congenial trail (1.2 miles, with pink markers) connects Bunker Hill Road, near its passage under I 83, with the Gunpowder South Trail near the Bunker Hill picnic area.

From east to west, the trail starts at a power pole on Bunker Hill Road about 100 yards west of the I 83 underpass and descends immediately into the woods. Crossing Bunker Hill Road .9 mile from the start, it ends at the Gunpowder South Trail near the Bunker Hill picnic area.

From west to east, the trail ascends from the Gunpowder South Trail, .1 mile southwest of the Bunker Hill picnic area, soon crosses Bunker Hill Road, and ends at Bunker Hill Road near I 83. Hikers continuing on the Mingo Forks Trail should cross Bunker Hill Road and follow the conspicuous track uphill.

Gunpowder North Trail

This trail (5.8 miles, with blue markers) lies north of Gunpowder Falls, extending from Big Falls Road to Falls Road. A major feature is Raven Rock Falls, a series of small cascades on a side stream .9 mile east of York Road (see map). To reach the entrances east and west of York Road, cross the guardrail at the twenty-seventh post (about fifty yards north) from the river, where the trail crosses the road. The entrance west of Big Falls Road is very close to the river, behind the bridge abutment, between a private driveway and the river. Cars must not be left on this driveway; instead, park beside the road, south of the river. Trail entrances on other roads can readily be found without special instructions.

Gunpowder South Trail

This trail (7.1 miles, with blue markers) lies south of Gunpowder Falls. It extends the full length of the Hereford Area of the park, from Big Falls Road to Prettyboy Dam, mostly on level ground close to the river. Particularly attractive stretches are between Big Falls Road and York Road and along the rugged section of the river above Falls Road. To begin at Prettyboy Dam, pass through a break in the wall at the southwest end of the parking lot southwest of the dam. As of 1982, parking at the dam and about half a mile either way along the road is forbidden on weekends and holidays; at other times it is limited to twenty minutes in the immediate vicinity of the dam. Observe the signs to avoid a stiff fine.

To begin at the entrance east of Masemore Road, cross Bush Cabin Run about fifty yards from the river, using large stones; if these are submerged because of high water, go up Masemore Road, cross Bush Cabin Run on the highway bridge, and return toward the river on the Masemore Link Trail (white markers).

From the entrance west of Bunker Hill Road at Camp Wood, the trail, marked by a signpost, goes up the hill behind the parking lot. After entering the woods, go straight down the hill, avoiding the Bunker Hill Trail, which follows an old road uphill to the left. All other entrances to the Gunpowder North Trail can readily be found; look for the blue markers at obvious places near the river.

Highland Trail

This trail (1.1 miles, with pink markers) connects the Gunpowder South Trail, near Masemore Road, with the same trail between Prettyboy Dam and Falls Road, offering you an alternative to retracing your steps along the river.

From east to west, the trail diverges from the Gunpowder South Trail just east of a brook, .1 mile west of Masemore Road, and ascends an old road. It turns right off the road before reaching a power line, drops to cross a brook, descends on the other side of the brook, and then climbs, going straight across the power-line clearing. Here the trail enters a service road, which it follows to Falls Road. After crossing Falls Road, the trail descends toward the

river, making a sharp right turn partway down, and reaches the
Gunpowder South Trail at a high point, about midway between
Falls Road and Prettyboy Dam.

From west to east, the trail leaves the Gunpowder South Trail at
the highest point above a hairpin turn in the river, about midway
between Falls Road and Prettyboy Dam. It ascends, crosses Falls
Road, enters a service road on the other side, and, almost immediately, bears left onto another service road. At the end of this road,
the trail goes straight across a power-line clearing and reenters the
woods. It descends a little and follows up the bank of a brook,
which it soon crosses. It then climbs and turns left onto an old road,
on which it descends to the Gunpowder South Trail, near Masemore Road.

Mingo Forks Trail

Mingo Branch, a tributary of Gunpowder Falls, was named after
the Mingo Indians, who used to come to this area from Pennsylvania. Parts of the Mingo Forks trail follow the east and west
forks of Mingo Branch. The trail (1.8 miles, with pink markers)
travels through some of the highest areas in the park, just south of
Bunker Hill Road. In places, open fields afford extensive views.

From east to west, the trail leaves Bunker Hill Road about one
hundred yards west of the passage under I 83, following a conspicuous track uphill. After paralleling I 83 behind a stand of pines
for .6 mile, it turns right, into the woods, in the middle of an
archery course (there is no danger to hikers). The trail crosses a
cleared lane .7 mile from the start and crosses the east fork of
Mingo Branch at .8 mile. After skirting the end of a ridge, it
ascends beside the attractive west fork of Mingo Branch, crossing it
at 1.1 miles. It then joins a park service road, climbs through a pine
grove, emerges into the open, and soon turns right (at 1.3 miles)
onto an old road. Follow this road to meet the Gunpowder South
Trail midway between Bunker Hill and Masemore roads.

From west to east, the trail departs toward the south, uphill from
the Gunpowder South Trail near the crest of a ridge midway
between Bunker Hill and Masemore roads. It first follows an old
road, from which it turns left half a mile from the start, before the
road goes through a hedgerow. The trail then descends toward a

large pine (avoiding a wide track farther to the left, which is sometimes mowed) and descends through a pine grove. At the end of the descent, bear left on a footpath (leaving the service road) and cross the west fork of Mingo Branch. The trail descends along the opposite bank, skirts a ridge, and crosses the east fork of Mingo Branch at 1.0 mile. It climbs to cross a cleared lane and emerges from the woods at 1.2 miles, in the middle of an archery course (there is no danger to hikers). Turning to the left, the trail ends at Bunker Hill Road, near I 83. The Bunker Hill Trail starts directly across Bunker Hill Road from the end of the Mingo Forks Trail.

Panther Branch Trail

This trail (2 miles, with pink markers), located south of Gunpowder Falls between Big Falls Road and York Road, swings over high ground well back from the river, traversing fields with open views. Along scenic Panther Branch, it passes the remains of several mill-wheel pits, earth dams, and fieldstone buildings. Its name is said to derive from a panther that long ago lived in a cave that is visible from the trail.

From east to west the trail leaves the Gunpowder South Trail thirty yards west of the Panther Branch crossing. It climbs over a ridge and returns to Panther Branch, which it follows for .6 mile. It then goes uphill, beside a pleasant brook, and crosses a field, a patch of woods, another field (sometimes planted with corn), and a dirt road. On the other side of the road, the trail passes through a hedgerow and turns right immediately onto another road. Follow this road past some pine plantings on the left and enter a section of hardwoods. After emerging from these woods, turn right on another road and, later, right again, after passing through another hedgerow. The trail soon reaches the top of the Sandy Lane Trail, 1.7 miles from the start. Avoid the fire lane that bears slightly left here and is sometimes mowed. Instead, make a sharp left, following the path with pink markers through a pine planting. The trail soon crosses a brook and eventually descends to join the Gunpowder South Trail near York Road.

From west to east, the Panther Branch Trail turns right off of the Gunpowder South Trail, just after the latter crosses a brook near York Road. It climbs to enter an old road, presently dips to a brook crossing, and soon bears right at the junction with the Sandy Lane Trail. After ascending gradually along various wood roads for another half mile, the trail reaches high terrain, with a pine planting on the right and a hedgerow on the left. Making a right-angled left turn through the hedgerow, it crosses a dirt road and a field, toward the right of a group of trees in the middle of the field. Beyond these trees, it crosses more of the field, enters the woods, and subsequently follows first a brook and then Panther Branch. It finally climbs over the end of a ridge and descends to the Gunpowder South Trail, near where it crosses Panther Branch.

Sandy Lane Trail

This short trail (.3 mile, with white markers) follows a wood road, connecting the Gunpowder South Trail, at a point 1.4 miles from York Road, with the Panther Branch Circuit, at a point half a mile from York Road.

Suggested Hikes

There are many ways the various trails can be followed, singly or in combination, for hikes of varying lengths. For easy introductions to the area, try the level walks along the Gunpowder North Trail, between Bunker Hill and Masemore roads or between Bunker Hill and York roads, and along the Gunpowder North and South trail, between Falls and Masemore roads.

The following descriptions are of longer circuit hikes.

Hike 7.1 Gunpowder Gorge Circuit

Easy 4.2-mile circuit, partly in a rock-strewn gorge through which flows the Gunpowder Falls; includes a spectacular view of the dam from below and an excursion over higher land.

Directions

Park at Masemore Road. Walk up the Gunpowder South Trail to Falls Road and continue to the foot of Prettyboy Dam. There are

Autumn stream scene (Bruce Van Alstine)

excellent lunch spots beside the fast water in the first half mile beyond Falls Road and on a large flat rock in the stream near the dam, 1.5 miles from the start. If time permits, go to the top of the dam to enjoy the fine view of the reservoir. Return downstream from the dam to the Highland Trail, which leaves the Gunpowder South Trail at its highest point above the river, at the first big bend below the dam. Ascend the Highland Trail (pink markers) and follow it west to east according to the detailed description given above. It ends at the Gunpowder South Trail, beside the river; turn right to return to the starting place.

Hike 7.2 Mingo Forks Circuit

Easy 3.8-mile circuit, traveling along woodland paths, beside attractive brooks, and over open fields with extended views; combines part of the Gunpowder South Trail with the Mingo Forks and Bunker Hill trails.

Directions

Park at the Camp Wood picnic area, south of Gunpowder Falls on Bunker Hill Road (see map). Take the Gunpowder South Trail (blue markers) up the hill behind the parking lot. After entering the woods, be careful to follow the Gunpowder South Trail down the hill, avoiding the Bunker Hill Trail (pink markers), which you will use on your return. Cross Mingo Branch, ascend to the top of a ridge, and continue to the junction with the Mingo Forks Trail. This junction is high on the ridge, .6 mile from the start. Turn left up the Mingo Forks Trail and follow it west to east, according to the detailed description given above; it ends at Bunker Hill Road. Cross the road and enter Bunker Hill Trail (pink markers). Descend this trail, crossing Bunker Hill Road again after .9 mile. On reaching the Gunpowder South Trail, turn right to the starting place at the picnic area.

Hike 7.3 Panther Branch Circuit

Moderate 5.4-mile circuit on woodland trails, along the river bank past Raven Rock Falls, up Panther Branch with its many old mill ruins, and through fields with open views.

Directions

Park on York Road, south of Gunpowder Falls. Enter the Gunpowder North Trail on the east side of the road, north of the river, by crossing the guardrail at the twenty-seventh post (about fifty yards) from the bridge. The trail descends slightly, climbs again, descends to the river, and passes beside a pasture. There is a very scenic lunch spot at Raven Rock Falls, .9 mile from the start. From here the trail follows the river, except for one detour over a ridge, 1.4 miles from the start, to avoid a marshy meadow and private land. On reaching Big Falls Road after 2.6 miles, cross the highway bridge and return upstream on the Gunpowder South Trail. Cross a brook .3 mile from Big Falls Road and then Panther Branch at .5 mile. Thirty yards beyond the latter crossing, turn left up the Panther Branch Trail (pink markers) and follow it east to west, according to the detailed description given above. When it joins the Gunpowder South trail near York Road, bear left to the starting point.

This hike can be shortened to 4.2 miles by taking the Gunpowder South Trail (instead of the Gunpowder North Trail) to the east end of the Panther Branch Trail (see map). A still shorter walk, of 2.2 miles, can be made by following the Gunpowder South Trail as far as the Sandy Lane Trail, and returning along it and the Panther Branch Trail.

8.   Oregon Ridge Park

Introduction to the Area

Shadowing the eastern end of Worthington Valley, the forested slopes of Oregon Ridge provide diverse opportunities for outdoor recreation. Oregon Ridge Park, owned and operated by the Baltimore County Department of Recreation and Parks, consists of 838 acres of mature woodlands and mowed fields.

There are two man-made ponds in the park: a four-acre, spring-fed ore pit known as Oregon Lake, and Ivy Hill Pond, which was created by damming a small tributary of Baisman Run. The southern half of the park drains to Baisman Run, while the northern half flows to the Oregon Branch of Beaver Dam Run. Both streams eventually reach Loch Raven Reservoir.

In the 1800s, Oregon Ridge was the site of iron ore mines, a blast furnace, and a mining town. Ore deposits were found where the Wissahickon schist of the ridge meets the Cockeysville marble of the valley floor. Ore was mined from three locations in the northwestern part of the park: the ore pit adjacent to the nature center, the lake, and the large depression east of the lake. Several buildings of the old Oregon mining town are still standing: the Oregon store, the mine overseer's house, a springhouse, the present park caretaker's house, the furnace foundation, a barn foundation, a stone barnyard, and two other company-town dwellings. These structures are located between the north slope of the ridge and the intersection of Shawan and Beaver Dam roads.

The park is the site of outdoor summer concerts, supervised swimming in a cool lake, cross-country skiing, picnicking, nature studies, hang-gliding, hiking, and many other family activities. The Oregon Ridge Lodge is a meeting place for a variety of community organizations.

The first county-sponsored nature center is located here. Development of nature trails is expected in the next few years. Existing trails, however, provide many opportunities for wildflower walks, bird-watching, insect study, photography, jogging, or just a lazy evening stroll.

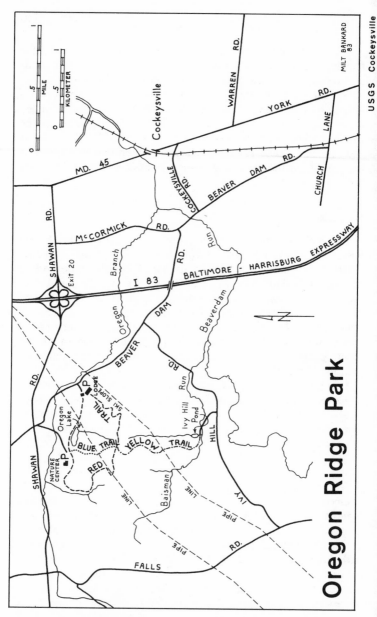

Oregon Ridge Park

USGS Cockeysville

MILT BANKARD
83

Trails at Oregon Ridge use abandoned logging roads and some recently established footpaths. Several of the steep logging roads are eroding; the exposed rock and soil provide poor footing during inclement weather. Portions of these older trails have been re-located to assure long-term stability of the trail system. There are three marked trails. They guide the hiker along circuits of the wooded ridge and down a spur to lovely Ivy Hill Pond, at the far end of the property. There are many unmarked trails in the woods for explorers; the straight pipe-line right-of-ways are ideal for novices.

Access

The park is open year-round from dawn until dusk. Oregon Ridge can easily be reached from I 83, north of the Baltimore Beltway. From Beltway Exit 24, follow I 83 north 5 miles to Exit 20 (Shawan Road). You will see a brown sign for the park before you reach the exit. Proceed west (away from the Hunt Valley complex) for 1 mile. Turn left onto Beaver Dam Road. The old stone Oregon Store building, built around 1850, is located on the corner. Immediately behind this building is the entrance road to the nature center parking area. Use caution when entering, since the gate may be closed.

To reach the lodge, continue southeast on Beaver Dam Road for a quarter of a mile. The gated entrance to the park is on the right, just beyond the mailbox that bears the park's name. Ample parking is available on the lot at the lodge. All trails can be reached from this vicinity.

Getting Lost

Once atop the ridge, you will see several side trails and old logging skid trails. Knowledge of the prominent features and layout of the park will be helpful should you stray from the trail. Two major natural gas transmission line rights-of-way cross the park from the southwest to the northeast. Heading northerly on either pipe line will bring you to the large open fields that border the northern side of the park, along Beaver Dam Road.

Park property is surrounded by residential homes and farms. To the east of the park is Ivy Hill Road; to the south and west is Falls Road. Walking north, you will arrive at Shawan Road (turn right) or Beaver Dam Road (look for the lodge). Your best insurance against getting lost is careful attention to the trail and the area around you. Look back occasionally.

Hike 8.1 Red Trail

Strenuous, 2.2-mile circuit to the ridge and back through diverse plant and wildlife communities; historic features; vista; shorter hikes possible; side trails; recommended year-round.

Trail's Attractions

The trail passes through a variety of forest, open land, and wetland wildlife habitats. The combination of abundant food, hiding places, and water results in optimal living conditions for many animals. White-tailed deer, red fox, raccoon, opossum, and eastern cottontail use this area. Look for their tracks in the snow that lingers at the base of this northern slope. The dense understory attracts yellowthroats, white-eyed vireos, rufous-sided towhees, wood thrushes, and brown thrashers. Watch for hawks soaring along this edge of the valley during fall migration. Bluebirds are common along the field edges.

The trail passes by the iron ore excavations, which were dug with pick and shovel in the 1800s. Overburden, material that had to be removed in order to reach the iron ore, formed the irregular mounds found here. The pit, just to the east of the pool, collects rainwater; spring rains bring a deafening evening chorus of spring peepers, American toads, wood frogs, and later in the season, the "ba-rump" of the bullfrog. If you are quiet, you may observe green herons feeding in the shallow waters of this pit. The scars of mining have been healed with yellow-poplars, black cherry trees, spice-bushes, sassafras, and Japanese honeysuckle, all of whose seeds were transported here by the wind and by birds.

This area of the park is the most heavily used on weekends, because of its proximity to the lodge and the lake. There are many places to spread a blanket and enjoy an afternoon picnic. Picnic tables and a shelter are available near the lake. Spring fed, the lake is also supplied, during dry periods, with water pumped from Oregon Branch. Historically, Oregon Lake has been used for fishing and swimming. In past winters, horse-drawn wagons were loaded with blocks of sawn ice from the lake, to be used in the refrigerators of nearby Cockeysville.

Trees found along the trail include white, black, scarlet, red, and chestnut oaks. Flowering dogwood and maple-leaved viburnum hide the deer that rest on these slopes. Before the appearance of the chestnut blight fungus in 1910, American chestnut was a common canopy tree here; stumps of this rot-resistant wood still remain along the trail. Because the roots of the chestnut trees are not killed by the fungus, they continue to sprout saplings, which survive for a few years before they succumb to the blight. Occasionally, saplings become sufficiently old to flower and produce the spiny burs that contain chestnuts. One such tree, now dead, may be found where the western portion of this trail meets the Atlantic Seaboard Corporation (ASC) pipe line right-of-way. In the forest, look for the chestnut saplings among the mountain laurel and pinxter azalea. You may hear ovenbirds, red-eyed vireos, and great-crested flycatchers as they forage for insects in this area.

Oxen dragging logs from these hillsides many years ago made the eroded trails that cross the path. Scars like these take a long time to heal. Unfortunately, some of these trails continue to be used, thus increasing the erosion problems caused by soil compaction.

At one point, a tributary to Oregon Branch borders the trail. A late winter walk will reveal a bright green stream border composed of skunk cabbage. In early May, look for violets (five species), rue anemone, mitrewort, trilliums, columbine, bluets, and broad beech fern. Along this section you will see small witch hazel trees, unusual in that their yellow, narrow-petaled flowers bloom in November. Watch for parula warblers, northern orioles, and Acadian flycatchers.

The forests on the dry ridges contain chestnut oaks, black huckleberry, early sweet blueberry, and mountain laurel. In the fall of 1981, strong winds toppled patches of canopy trees near the path. Search for the rectangular holes of the pileated woodpecker in the fallen debris. Lightning damage is visible on trees near the highest point in the park (630 feet), located near the ASC right-of-way.

The forests of the ridge are about sixty-five years old. In places, the trees are over one hundred feet high. On the wooded ridges you will find blackgum, pignut hickory, and red maple trees. Other plants in the area include bellwort, false Solomon's seal, rattlesnake fern, bloodroot, showy orchids, trumpet honeysuckle, and American hazelnut. Poison ivy occurs infrequently along the path, so beware.

At the top of the ski slope, take a break to enjoy the vista. The building on the distant ridge is the Farm Credit Bank of Baltimore, located at Loveton Business Center.

In the valley and along the ridge the trail is gently rolling. Several places on the ascent and descent have relatively steep grades and become slippery during inclement weather.

Directions

The Red Trail is a circuit trail that begins and ends at the lodge. It begins west of the lodge, at the corner of the tennis court. Look for the Red Trail marker. Proceeding away from the lodge, the trail passes through an open grove of black locust and black cherry trees. At the far end of the grove is the grassy ASC pipe line right-of-way. Walk 150 feet uphill and cross the right-of-way. Descend the log stairs in the gap at the edge of the woods. To your left is Oregon Lake and to your right is another abandoned ore pit. Climb the small embankment and cross the open lawn, passing to the left of the bathhouse. Beyond the beach and pavilion, climb the stony access road and bear left, into the woods, at the corner of the nature center parking lot.

A short distance into the woods, you will find the beginning of the Blue Trail; it leads uphill to the left. Continue on the Red Trail, which dips slightly as it crosses a drainage area filled with spicebush. As the grade increases, the nature center and iron ore pit will come into view on your right. At the inconspicuous fork, bear right, down the incline. (The left fork rejoins the Red Trail [right fork] on the ridge, but it is steep, eroding, and less attractive.) The path curves to the left, paralleling a tributary of Oregon Branch, and climbs to reach the ridge at a T intersection. (The left fork mentioned above connects here, from the left). Turn right and proceed along the ridge to the pipe line right-of-way. Cross the right-of-way, turn right, and follow the edge three hundred feet, to a path entering the woods on the left. Look for the bellwort on this corner, as you turn left onto this trail. Not far into the woods, a short cut to the Yellow Trail exits to the right. At this intersection is a hazelnut shrub. Continue straight. The Yellow Trail connects from the right and, a little later, the Blue Trail joins from the left.

Look for the huge spreading yellow-poplar on the north side of the trail in this segment. A steep, eroding trail will join on the left. Continue along the ridge until you see the clearings of the upper ski slope on the left. Turn left, leaving the ridge logging road. The top of the ski slope has a scenic view and is a nice rest stop.

Return to the lodge via the trail that enters the forest at the top of the slope; it will be on your left as you face downhill. The trail has a moderate grade and is negotiable in winter on cross-country skis. It meanders and crosses several log-drag trails. Stay on the marked trail until it exits on the grassy knoll behind the lodge.

When taking this trail in the opposite direction, begin at the entrance on the grassy bench directly behind the lodge. Do not use the trail located in the ravine to the right.

Hike 8.2 Blue Trail

Strenuous, direct .4-mile route to the ridge; connects with other trails at terminus; woodland flowers; recommended in spring, summer, and fall.

Trail's Attractions

This trail is the most direct route from the Oregon Lake area to the top of the ridge. It is a continuously climbing trail, with several grades greater than 10 percent. The steepness of the trail makes it slippery following heavy summer rains and winter ice and snow.

The lower end of the trail is within the disturbed terrain of the mined iron ore pits. The plant community here consists of yellow-poplar, black locust, and red maple trees above blackberries, spicebushes, and Japanese honeysuckle. Nearby are pale violets, greater celandine, wineberry, Virginia creeper, and bedstraw. Watch for poison ivy here.

Where the grade steepens, logs have been placed as steps. Sunlight comes through the canopy above the trail in places, warming the sandy soil patches found by each step. Iridescent green tiger beetles nest in these sunny patches. Halfway up the slope, the canopy is made up of black, white, and chestnut oaks. In the understory, look for mountain laurel, early sweet blueberry, American chestnut, maple-leaved viburnum, blackgum, and flowering dogwood.

At the gas pipe line right-of-way, watch downhill for deer, indigo buntings perched along the forest's edge, and a variety of butterflies, beetles, and bees feeding on the Joe-pye weed and goldenrod. In the summer, you can pick blackberries here.

This is an old established trail, dating from Oregon Ridge's logging era, prior to the 1900s. The easiest way to bring the huge logs down this hillside was to hitch them to oxen and drag them along the ridge line and down to the valley—the most direct route possible. Repeated travels along these routes resulted in well-established ravines, such as those found along this trail.

The steep shaded banks of the ravines do not allow falling leaves to collect and develop into the rich humus characteristic of the forest floor. Consequently, the shaded dirt banks are colonized by primitive plants such as lichens, mosses, and ferns. Look here for New York, hay-scented, and interrupted ferns. At the rim of the fragile banks you may find wild sarsaparilla, mountain-mint, false Solomon's seal, pink lady slippers, rue anemone, rattlesnake plantain, four-leaved milkweed, whorled loosestrife, and partridgeberry.

The oak-covered hillsides are the homes of raccoons, gray squirrels, red-eyed vireos, ovenbirds, scarlet tanagers, blue jays, great-crested flycatchers, red-bellied woodpeckers, and white-breasted nuthatches. Listen for the wood peewee as it sings its name.

Directions

The Blue Trail begins in the nature center parking lot, at the corner nearest to Oregon Lake. If the access road to the nature center is closed, you can reach this location by taking the Red Trail west from the lodge (half a mile).

You should have no difficulty following the Blue Trail. Beginning at the junction of the Red and Blue trails, the Blue Trail ascends a slight, but steadily increasing, grade. The trail has widely spaced log steps which function very poorly in diverting water from the trail but which have been somewhat beneficial in stabilizing the path. Winding back and forth, the trail follows the shallow ravines of the log-dragging scars. Where it crosses the pipe line right-of-way, you can look on one side of the trail, down a steep slope to a stream, and, on the other side, up the slope toward the ridge. Beyond the right-of-way, the ravine becomes deeper and the grade increases. Keep off the banks of the ravine, as the plant communities there are fragile. The trail curves slowly to the right and becomes level as it approaches the ridge. On the ridge it rejoins the Red Trail. Within sight of this junction is the Yellow Trail, which leads to Ivy Hill Pond. Turn left on the Red Trail to reach the lodge and right to reach the nature center.

Hike 8.3 Yellow Trail

Moderately strenuous; .8 mile; flat ridge and stream valley; trout pond, stream; access via Hike 8.1 or 8.2; side trails; nonnative and indigenous plantings; recommended year-round.

Trail's Attractions

This path takes the hiker from the Red Trail, on the ridge, to the south end of the park, at Ivy Hill Road. Ivy Hill Pond and the adjacent plantings were developed by the previous owners, Mr. and Mrs. H. Lee Hoffman, noted conservationists.

Near the pond you will see rhododendrons, privet, leucothoë, hemlock, and white birch. The azaleas along the path are in full bloom in mid-May. Throughout the springtime, the pond bustles with the activity of wood frogs, spotted salamanders, red-spotted newts, painted turtles, and green herons. Below the pond is Baisman Run, which contains brook trout, blacknose dace, creek chubs, and crayfish. Aquatic insects are abundant under the stream rocks.

The walk along the gently rolling terrain of the ridge top passes through mature forest, where yellow-poplars dominate the canopy. The understory contains flowering dogwood, maple-leaved viburnum, American beech, pignut hickory, chinquapin, and the spiny Hercules' club. Along the trail are showy orchids, *Collinsonia,* pennywort, trumpet honeysuckle, bellwort, bedstraw, and Indian cucumber-root.

During spring migration flocks of purple finches and goldfinches pass through these treetops, stopping to feed on yellow poplar seeds. Later, you may see black-throated blue warblers, parula warblers, and rose-breasted grosbeaks eating buds and insects in the treetops. In the late summer, young-of-the-year birds feed in these woods before their long migration south.

Directions

Access to this trail is possible from the Blue Trail (.4 mile), which begins at the nature center parking lot, or from the Red Trail (.7 mile), starting from the lodge. The Yellow Trail begins where the end of the Blue Trail meets the Red Trail.

Located on a well-defined forest road, the Yellow Trail is easy to follow. From the intersection of the Red and Blue trails, it heads toward the south over gently rolling terrain. The trail bends slowly to the left and passes through a barely noticeable depression just above the headwaters of the stream that feeds Ivy Hill Pond. Beyond this depression the trail straightens. Midway along this stretch, another trail joins obliquely from the right. It leads to the Red Trail, near the A.S.C. pipe line. Continuing to follow the Yellow Trail markers, make a wide right turn followed by a slightly sharper left. The clearing here is the right-of-way for the Transco gas pipe line. A side trip up or down the pipe line will add to the variety of plants and wildlife you can see in this area. Cross the pipe line and follow the trail as it bends slowly to the right. You will soon observe plantings of rhododendron and azalea bordering the trail. Another trail intersects perpendicularly on the left. Continue between the azaleas. The trail steepens and curves left as it descends into the stream valley of Baisman Run. When you reach the stream level, the small boulder dam of Ivy Hill Pond is on your left. Take a break, explore the pond area, and return by the same route.

9. Loch Raven Reservoir

Introduction to the Area

Loch Raven is the Baltimore City reservoir closest to Baltimore's population center. The popular Fishing Center is located here, not far from a picnic area with tables for hundreds of people. Hikers and amateur naturalists may use the many miles of maintenance and fire-road trails in the less well-known, less heavily used, and remarkably well-preserved natural woodlands and planted pine forests surrounding the lake.

Loch Raven Reservoir, created by the damming of the Gunpowder Falls, is quite different from the other city reservoirs. The underlying rock strata of the area are eastern piedmont metasedimentary rocks, predominantly Cockeysville marble. Gently sloping banks and other shoreline characteristics make the area a good fish and waterfowl (surface and bottom-feeding) habitat; the lake serves as a migratory flyway stopover for ducks and geese. The rolling lands bordering the lake contain varied wildlife habitats and many unusual natural attractions.

The Fishing Center at Loch Raven is operated by the Baltimore County Department of Recreation and Parks. You can rent boats and purchase fishing licenses here. To reach the center, take Dulaney Valley Road north from the Beltway (Exit 27) about 4.5 miles. For information regarding rates and operating hours, call (301) 252–8755.

Loch Raven Reservoir, run by the Baltimore City Bureau of Engineering (Water Division), is the oldest of the three Baltimore City reservoirs still in operation. It covers approximately 2,400 acres, and the city owns 5,600 acres of land surrounding it (referred to as watershed lands), of which 4,533 acres are in natural woodlands and the remaining acres have been planted with several varieties of pine. First established in 1881, the reservoir was enlarged in 1912 and again in the early 1920s, when it reached its present size. At the time of the enlargements, the Gunpowder Falls Valley was settled, with many small communities, mills, and

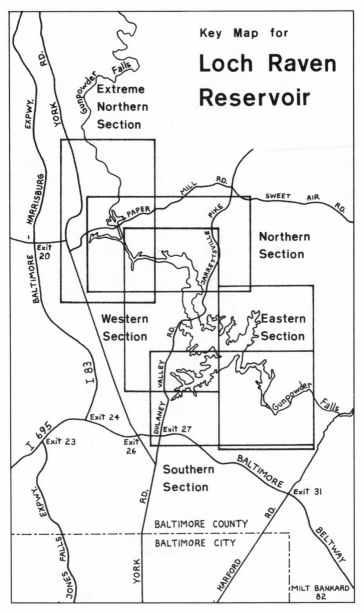

Key Map for

Loch Raven
Reservoir

Extreme Northern Section

Northern Section

Western Section

Eastern Section

Southern Section

BALTIMORE COUNTY
BALTIMORE CITY

93

country mansions and estates, some of which were inundated. In many places, vestiges of these settlements are visible along the shore. Numerous small family plots (or cemeteries) mark the locations of former estates and farms. Neighboring communities, as well as some trails, take their names from the former estates. Some early nineteenth-century mansions in the area have been preserved.

Hikers on the Loch Raven watershed trails should realize that they are enjoying a privilege. In some other communities, recreational use of municipal water supply lands is not permitted; hikers are rarely allowed free access to so many miles of trails. They should, therefore, have a heightened sense of responsibility about the land and waters.

Public use of the Loch Raven watershed lands is now heavy and is certain to increase in the future; the value of these lands as scenic, educational, and hiking resources, as well as their importance for the protection of water quality, will become more apparent as time passes. The bureau's land protection policies have been threatened in the past and will be again, unless the public gives its support. The bureau now operates with no support for this unofficial part of its program—the preservation of wildlands—and with very limited funds for supervision, patrol, and enforcement of its regulations for recreational use.

If you enjoy the watershed lands, you have an obligation to help preserve them for the future, both by using them wisely and by voicing support for the policies that established and now maintain them. Call or write the Bureau of Engineering (Water Division) or the mayor to express your interest. See Chapter 1 for information about citizen involvement in upkeep of trails and policy support.

Regulations

The Baltimore City Bureau of Engineering has several regulations that must be observed if the public is to retain access to its land. Pollution of the waters of the reservoirs or their tributaries is prohibited. Use the sanitary facilities that are provided near the fishing and picnicking areas. You are not permitted to skate, build fires, park or drive vehicles (including motorcycles) except on surfaced roads, swim or wade, or use firearms. Boating is allowed only by permit, and fishing licenses are required. No camping is permitted. Remember that this is a nature preserve; leave all wildflowers for others to see and enjoy, and pick up your luncheon debris.

Access to the Loch Raven Reservoir Area

Hikes in Loch Raven are all between five and twenty minutes' driving time from the Baltimore Beltway; most are within half an hour's drive from the city's center. To reach the entrances to these trails, use any of Beltway Exits 24, 26, 27, or 28; check the hike descriptions for suggested access routes to individual trails.

Getting Lost

Getting lost on a watershed trail should not be easy; however, if you do get lost, you should have little difficulty reorienting yourself. The watershed boundaries are usually marked—by private landowners' barbed-wire fences and occasionally by Bureau of Engineering signs. Since the trails rim a valley, homes and roads are always nearby on the uphill side. Make use of the maps as well as the trail descriptions to avoid getting lost.

Hike 9.1 Deadman's Cove Circuit

Easy 2-mile circuit through woods and along interesting shoreline; recommended for families as well as for other hikers; especially good in winter.

Trail's Attractions

Watershed lands in the vicinity of Deadman's Cove differ from other watershed lands. They include open fields, frequent low-lying limestone outcroppings, sparse deciduous and evergreen woods with occasional stunted trees, and large groves of native cedars. Features of the landscape here are splendid views of the lake and cove and extensive beachlike shorelines.

Even families taking small children on their first wildlands trip can see wildlife at first hand on Deadman's Cove Circuit. You can see deer tracks in all seasons, and with luck, you may spot a deer. Ducks often touch down in Deadman's Cove, and hikers who wait quietly in the cove area will almost certainly see the resident family of belted kingfishers and hear the kingfishers' loud jackhammer call. Overhead you will see circling turkey vultures and, perhaps, a red-tailed hawk.

Woods and field wildflowers, such as violets, bluets, everlasting, and pussytoes, are abundant. Wild strawberries grow in the more open spaces and are ripe in June. There are several small streams like the one entering the cove, along whose moist banks, in springtime, you can find such wildflowers as skunk cabbage, May-apple, and Jack-in-the-pulpit, as well as several kinds of ferns.

You may enjoy walking along the shoreline, where the earth and the rocks have been weathered by the elements, creating interesting patterns.

Deadman's Cove is a popular fishing spot, so the trail is fairly heavily used. Unfortunately, parts of the trail are spoiled by traffic noise from Dulaney Valley Road. In spite of these distractions, the hike is pleasurable at any time. Many of its wildlife attractions and the interesting and scenic shoreline may be more enjoyable, however, on a winter's day, when you are more likely to find quiet and isolation in the cove.

Directions

From Beltway Exit 27, take Dulaney Valley Road (Md. 146) north 3.3 miles to a small parking pull-out on the right side of the road (there are pull-outs on the left, too). This parking area is .4 mile beyond the Stella Maris private drive (which is on the left), at the point where roadside trees change from planted pines to deciduous woods. The trail entrance is marked by a bureau sign and fence posts. It is not safe to turn around in the road here, so always park to your right. When you leave, if you need to turn around, drive on until you reach a safe place to do so.

The trail is not a true circuit, as it entails following the road for a short distance. Two trails lead off from the entrance: a wide, grassy fire road to the right and an inviting, long-abandoned road to the left. As the two trails are parallel, connecting in several places, it is

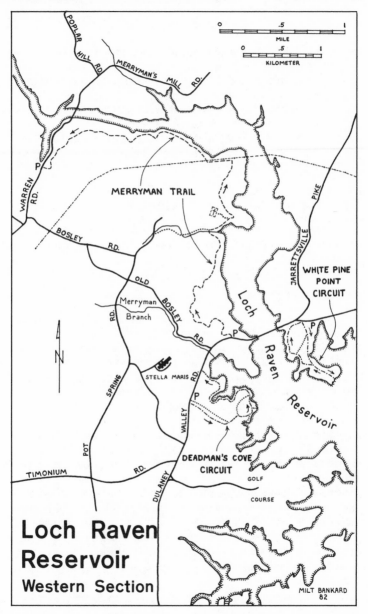

Loch Raven Reservoir
Western Section

MERRYMAN TRAIL

WHITE PINE POINT CIRCUIT

DEADMAN'S COVE CIRCUIT

POPLAR HILL RD.

MERRYMAN'S MILL RD.

WARREN RD.

BOSLEY RD.

OLD BOSLEY RD.

Merryman Branch

SPRING RD.

STELLA MARIS

VALLEY RD.

POT

TIMONIUM RD.

DULANEY

JARRETTSVILLE PIKE

Loch Raven Reservoir

GOLF COURSE

MILT BANKARD 82

MILE
KILOMETER

N

97

possible to take either one or a combination of both. Take the fire
road to the water's edge and follow the shoreline around Deadman's Cove to a small fishermen's trail that leads to Dulaney
Valley Road. This trail is heavily overgrown in some places and is
difficult to follow. Because the trail is close to the shore, you can
cut over and walk along the beach when the trail is impassable,
returning to the trail when it clears. Upon reaching the highway,
turn left and, staying on the same side of the road and watching for
traffic, return to the trail entrance.

Hike 9.2 White Pine Point Circuit

Easy, pleasant 1.5-mile circuit good for families and
bird-watchers; recommended all year except during fishing
season.

Trail's Attractions

White Pine Point Circuit is named after the white pines on the tip
of the peninsula. These trees, unusually tall for this area, block
most of the sun's rays, so that only sparse underbrush grows on the
forest floor; the distance between the canopy and the underbrush
creates a cool, airy cavern. The trail passes through deciduous
woods and young pine fields full of weeds and of birds eating the
weed seeds. It also follows the shoreline in several places. From the
east side of the peninsula, you may see wading birds feeding at the
mouth of the stream that enters the lake across the water, below
Dulaney Valley Road. From a vantage point hidden in the pines on
the point, you may see migrating waterfowl feeding and resting just
offshore.

Bird-watching along the shoreline on White Pine Point is often
unrewarding during the fishing season, because of the number of
fishermen in the area; most aspects of this hike are less enjoyable at
this time of year. At all other times, you will find this a lovely
setting for a pleasant walk. There are many beautiful views of the
reservoir, and mountain laurel, dogwood, and wildflowers abound
along the trail.

Directions

From Beltway Exit 27, take Dulaney Valley Road (Md. 146) north approximately 4 miles, to the first turn-off on the right after passing the bridge over Loch Raven Reservoir and the entrance to Jarrettsville Pike (on the left). At the junction of Dulaney Valley Road and Jarrettsville Pike, Dulaney Valley Road turns right and descends a hill. Immediately beyond this turn you will see a sign on the right that says No Parking Dusk to Dawn. The trail entrance, easily missed, is near this sign on the other side of the guard rail.

The circuit is not difficult to follow. Take the dirt fire road to the point and follow the footpath around to the west side of the peninsula.

Hike 9.3 Merryman

Moderate 5-mile (one-way) hike, or easy circuits of 5 and 3 miles; scenic shoreline footpaths and woodland wild-flower trails; recommended for families and for all hikers, in all seasons.

Trail's Attractions

Merryman Trail's terrain and lake vistas are as beautiful and varied as any you will find in the Loch Raven Reservoir area. Several hikes are possible here, and they lend themselves, separately or in combination, to lingering nature study or to vigorous hiking.

Several streams chock-full of lush wildflowers and ferns cross the trail. Pawpaws grow near the shoreline—a rare treat in this locale. Near the middle of the hike is an exceptionally tall, dense forest of tulip poplars, remarkable because so much timber in the region is of relatively new growth. The wide vista of Loch Raven that you can see from rocky Merryman's Point is a major attraction and should be included whatever combination of trails you follow. The shoreline north of the point is forested with mixed hardwoods interlaced with dogwoods, mountain laurels, and ferns.

Near Dulaney Valley Road, the shoreline path is sometimes

marred by traffic noise; many popular fishing spots are also located along this section of shore. As a result, you will not find here the isolation, quiet, and remoteness that characterize the trail beyond the power line. Housing developments of close-packed homes near the middle section of the trail will also diminish the trail's wild-lands character in coming years; this section will thus serve as an example of the ill effects of the lack of buffer zoning. Interested citizens should encourage the county to protect its park areas with proper zoning.

Directions

From Beltway Exit 27, take Dulaney Valley Road (Md. 146) north 3.9 miles, to a parking place and the trail entrance. This wide, graveled pull-out is half a mile north of Old Bosley Road. There is ample parking space for fifteen cars. The trail entrance, marked by two metal posts with a connecting cable, is visible from here. On the left is the fire-road trail; straight ahead is the fisherman's path, which leads to the nearby water's edge.

To hike the full length of the trail from Dulaney Valley Road to Warren Road, follow the fire-road trail until it crosses a little run that widens to form a beautiful, deep ravine down toward the water's edge. After crossing the run, the trail intersects an old roadbed. Turn right and follow the old roadbed downhill, to the cutoff that leads to the Merryman family cemetery. A short dis-tance beyond the cemetery cutoff you will see, on your right, the trail to the point. You can either continue on the main trail or take this short spur for a good view of Loch Raven Reservoir. Con-tinuing on the main trail (the fire road), you come to the power-line cut, a wide, grassy swath along the power line. Walk uphill on the cut. About thirty yards beyond the second tower, the fire road goes into the woods on your right; follow it to Warren Road. Midway between the power line and Warren Road you will enter a very steep and beautiful ravine in which there is a break of several hundred yards in the fire road. Take the footpath up the ravine about 150 yards until you reach a rock that rises about two feet from the middle of the trail. Cross the stream on your right at this point. Follow a footpath several hundred yards to the fire road and take the fire road to Warren Road.

You can make a 3-mile circuit hike near Dulaney Valley Road by first following the fire road and then returning along the shoreline footpath. To reach the shoreline footpath, just before the old road and ravine, it is necessary to bushwhack for a few hundred yards down to the path. To make a longer circuit, you can add the smaller (2-mile) loop beyond Merryman's Point.

If you do not hike the whole trail in one day, you may want to devote a separate day's hike to the section near Warren Road and the short footpath that follows the stream bed to the shore. There is plenty of parking space along Warren Road, and the trail is an easily found fire road about .3 mile past the intersection of Warren and Bosley roads.

Hike 9.4 Overshot Run

Easy 3-mile (one-way), excellent bird and wildflower walk; passes stream with many waterfalls; recommended in all seasons.

Trail's Attractions

Overshot Run is so fine a nature trail as to make an amateur naturalist out of almost anyone. It is a relaxing, easy hike, on a good trail bed. Lovely wildflower-lined Overshot Run, with its many waterfalls upstream, and the entire central section of the trail are quiet and untouched, remarkably isolated from the surrounding settlements.

The trail runs through several different plant and animal habitats. Near Jarrettsville Pike is a rocky, steeply sloping deciduous woods, sprinkled with dogwoods, mountain laurels, and spice-bushes, whose beautiful colors enliven the woods in spring. You will recognize here the mitten-shaped leaf of the sassafras tree, from whose roots sassafras tea is made. On the forest floor are many permanent three-foot-high ant hills of the Pennsylvania mound-building ant. The green tiger beetle, which is a characteristic inhabitant of most of these woods trails, is conspicuous here.

The trail descends into the Overshot Run Valley, which is low and swampy and hosts a multitude of different spring and summer wildflowers and birds. Jack-in-the-pulpit, skunk cabbage (most fragrant when accidentally crushed underfoot), and handsome hellebore will be found in the moist places near springs and streams. In early spring a winter wren was spotted here. One late spring day, over thirty-five species of bird were seen or heard, including hooded warblers, kingfishers, blue-gray gnatcatchers, and a brood of quail right beside the path. If you approach the run quietly, you may surprise a great blue heron feeding in the shallows.

Near Merryman's Mill Road is a somewhat open area, over-grown with red cedar and pine, and deciduous woods with beech, ash, dogwood, and a few specimens of post oak and redbud. In late spring, this end of the trail is white with blackberry and strawberry blossoms and ox-eye daisies. At several points paths lead down to the water's edge from the trail. Near Merryman's Mill Road a wide expanse of Loch Raven Reservoir is visible from the main trail; you may see ducks and geese resting or feeding offshore, and an osprey may dive overhead. During fishing season the lakeshore at this point is frequented by fishermen, but in later afternoon you may find it empty and quiet. Ducks float offshore here often, seemingly oblivious to human presence.

There is a minor trash problem at the end of the trail, but the greatest detracting element is that motorcyclists frequently ride on the section near Jarrettsville Pike. The Bureau of Engineering prohibits the use of motorcycles on unpaved trails. Besides de-stroying the tranquility of the watershed area, motorcycles are destructive to the trails. The city needs citizen support to aid in handling this problem.

Overshot Run Trail can provide a strenuous 6-mile hike (round trip) or a leisurely stroll. The trail is fairly level until it crosses Overshot Run, about a mile from the entrance. Walking to the run and back is pleasant and easy. To hike farther, cross the run on a log and follow the trail as it climbs steeply and then winds along a ridge to Jarrettsville Pike. Parking is more plentiful and safer at the Merryman's Mill Road, so begin there unless you are organizing a car shuttle.

Directions

From Beltway Exit 27, follow Dulaney Valley Road north about 4 miles to a fork in the road, where Jarrettsville Pike leads to the left

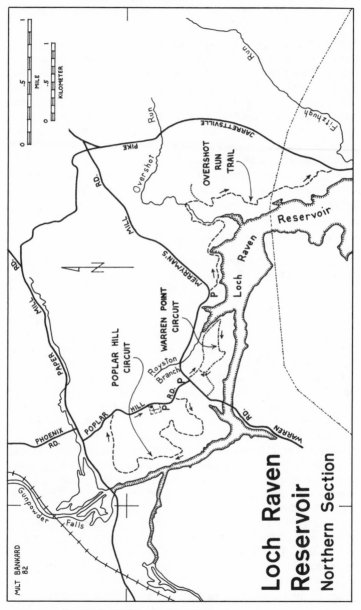

Loch Raven Reservoir
Northern Section

OVERSHOT RUN TRAIL

WARREN POINT CIRCUIT

POPLAR HILL CIRCUIT

Loch Raven Reservoir

Royston Branch

Overshot Run

Fitzhugh Run

JARRETTSVILLE PIKE

MERRYMAN'S MILL RD.

PAPER MILL RD.

PHOENIX RD.

POPLAR HILL RD.

WARREN RD.

Gunpowder Falls

MILT BANKARD 82

MILE

KILOMETER

N

(just past a bridge over Loch Raven Reservoir). Drive on Jarrettsville Pike about 1 mile. The trail entrance is opposite a shingle
house on the right. For a shuttle hike, leave shuttle cars at the small
pull-out just beyond the house. Continue on Jarrettsville Pike about
3 miles to Merryman's Mill Road (Warren Road). Turn left onto
Merryman's Mill Road and drive 1.6 miles to an unmarked dirt fire
road on the left side, about 150 yards before you can see the
lakeshore from the road. Parking for many cars is available along
the shoulder on both sides of the road.

The trail leads downhill and is easy to follow all the way. Hikers
desiring a longer hike may follow nearby Poplar Hill Circuit or the
adjacent trails at Warren Point.

Hike 9.5 Warren Point Circuit

Easy, 2-mile woodland circuit, with scenic viewpoint;
recommended in all seasons.

Trail's Attractions

Warren Point Circuit is a short woodland hike around and over a
small, hilly peninsula located at the northern end of Loch Raven
Reservoir, where Gunpowder Falls widens to form the reservoir.
The terrain and vegetation of the peninsula are varied and interesting. The trail leads from the periphery of low-lying open fields,
marshlands, and the water's edge to the high rocky ridge in the
middle. Rising abruptly about two hundred feet, the ridge is
covered with dense, tall, mixed hardwoods and mountain laurel.

Warren Point Circuit and its many sidepaths provide a rewarding
opportunity for nature observation and exploration. If you are
interested in a more strenuous, all-day hike, you can easily combine this circuit with adjacent Overshot Run Trail or Poplar Hill
Circuit, without having to move a car.

The suggested clockwise circuit forms a closed M shape. Selected from a labyrinth of fire roads in various states of maintenance
and disuse, these trails can be confusing, especially in seasons
when the trees are in leaf and the overgrowth lush. You will never
be far from clearly defined boundaries, however, so reorienting
yourself should not be difficult. Merryman's Mill Road and Cam-

bria III (a housing development beyond the road) are to the west and north, Royston Run, an inlet, and a vast expanse of the reservoir are to the northeast and east, and Gunpowder Falls runs to the south.

Directions

From Beltway Exit 24, take I 83 north 2 miles to the turnoff to Padonia Road. Turn right and drive about .8 mile to York Road. Turn left (north) on York Road and follow it about 1.4 miles to Warren Road (at a traffic signal). After turning right (east) on Warren Road, pass the settlement of Warren and cross Warren Road Bridge. East of the bridge, Warren Road is also known as Merryman's Mill Road. Turn left on Poplar Hill Road, just beyond the bridge, and park at the first pull-out.

The trail entrance is opposite Poplar Hill Road on Merryman's Mill Road and is marked by two metal posts with a connecting wire cable. At the entrance, the trail is an open, wide fire road. To begin, walk straight ahead. Another trail soon comes in from the right. Note this, for it will be your return trail at the end of the hike. Continue on the main trail (left fork), which then comes close to the inlet's shore. Follow it until the trail makes a sudden acute-angle switchback to the right and goes steeply uphill to the crest of the ridge. You may make this turn now or come back to it later, if you prefer to continue straight ahead on the wide fishermen's path to the shoreline. Once on top of the ridge, the main trail branches into two paths. The path to the right follows the ridge westward; the left path leads to the south, down the other side of the ridge. Take the trail leading south down the side of the ridge. There will be several more turns, but the trail is easily followed. As you head back toward the trail entrance, keep bearing left. There are two ridge fire roads coming in from the right and one coming in from the left. Stay on the main trail.

Hike 9.6 Poplar Hill Circuit

Pleasant, easy, 3-mile woodland circuit in a relatively isolated area; recommended in all seasons.

Trail's Attractions

Poplar Hill Circuit, the northernmost Loch Raven watershed trail, is situated where the valley sides close in on the river. This beautiful circuit is cool and shady in summer and has fine distant views of the valley in other seasons. Although the terrain is hilly, the trail is level. It curves around, but not into, two steep ravines along the crest of a ridge, about two hundred feet above the river. The woodlands here are made up of tall, dense, deciduous trees. There is quiet and a feeling of remoteness unusual on a Loch Raven watershed hike.

The trail is clear and easy to follow for its entire length. At several points old logging skids, which look like faint trails, intersect the trail. Although they reach only part way to the water's edge, from their terminations you can bushwhack to the shoreline. The footpath in the rocky area near the stream is especially rewarding. Mountain laurel is abundant, and at the mouth of the stream, there is a marshy area with many natural attractions. In some seasons you can cross the stream and find your way back to the trail on the other side of the ravine. The rocky, steep slopes have a very sparse ground cover and are easy to bushwhack through. At the trail's end in late summer you will receive a bonus—large, luscious, wild grapes.

Directions

Follow the directions given for Hike 9.5 to reach Poplar Hill Road. Turn left onto Poplar Hill Road and drive .3 mile, noting the post-and-rail fencing on the right, around private property. About one hundred yards farther, directly across from the private property on the left, is a trail entrance, marked by two metal posts and a connecting cable. Parking is available at the old Poplar Grove Methodist Church, a short distance beyond the trail entrance.

Hike 9.7 Jessops Circuit

Easy, scenic 2-mile nature trail in isolated area; good for watching waterfowl; recommended in all seasons.

Trail's Attractions

Jessops Circuit is a choice, short nature trail with a variety of scenery and wildlife habitat. The woods are a mixture of deciduous and evergreen trees, and all the common woodland wildflowers are represented. The little camel's hump (peninsula) on which the circuit is situated is quiet, remote, beautiful, and undisturbed. Views over the Jessop Valley and Gunpowder Falls are breathtaking when trees are not in leaf. The view from the boulders at the confluence of Beaverdam and Western runs is particularly nice; this would be a good lunch spot. The marshlands between Jessops and Phoenix circuits are long-time migratory waterfowl stops, for Canada and snow geese as well as for many species of duck. You may see shore and wading birds here as well. The best vantage point for observing the waterfowl is probably the Paper Mill Road bridge over Gunpowder Falls.

The land north and south of Paper Mill Road belonged to the Jessops family in the early 1800s. Kenilworth, the brick home on Towson Nursery land, west of the railroad, and Ivanhoe, the brick home just east of the railroad, are both Jessop houses, built in the early nineteenth century. High on the hill (at the northern, back edge of Towson Nursery land), you can see the old Jessop Methodist Church—one of the oldest in the country—whose entrance is on York Road. The little cemetery just east of Ivanhoe, on city land, is an old Jessops family plot.

Vandalism plagues the cemetery, and the bend in the abandoned macadam-surfaced section of Paper Mill Road near the trail entrance is marred by dumping and other trash left after parties. Citizens must convince the city and county that there is widespread interest in eradicating these and similar nuisances.

Directions

From Beltway Exit 24 take I 83 north 5 miles to the Shawan Road exit; turn right (east) on Shawan Road and drive 1 mile to York Road. Turn right (south) on York Road and drive .3 mile to Ashland Road, which enters only on your left. Follow Ashland Road .4 mile to a fork in the road and take the left fork, which is

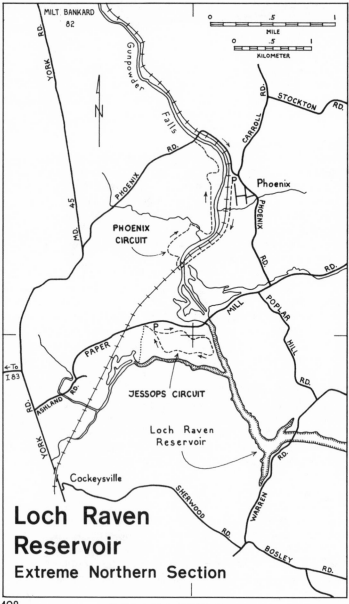

MILT. BANKARD
82

Gunpowder Falls

YORK RD.

MD. 45

PHOENIX RD.

**PHOENIX
CIRCUIT**

CARROLL RD.

STOCKTON RD.

P

Phoenix

PHOENIX RD.

RD.

MILL

POPLAR

HILL

RD.

P

PAPER

JESSOPS CIRCUIT

←To
I 83

YORK RD.

ASHLAND RD.

Loch Raven
Reservoir

RD.

Cockeysville

WARREN RD.

SHERWOOD RD.

BOSLEY RD.

0 ———— .5 ———— 1
MILE

0 ———— .5 ———— 1
KILOMETER

N

Loch Raven
Reservoir
Extreme Northern Section

Paper Mill Road. The parking place is .8 mile from the fork, just beyond the railroad overpass. There is a macadam pull-off on the right, with metal posts and room for as many as four cars.

You can see the trail and a spur path from this parking area, as well as an old macadam road which is no longer used. The trail bears to the right about thirty yards from the parking area, and the old macadam road leads to the left. After about twenty-five yards, the trail bears to the left, and you will see a spur path to the river on the right. Follow the main trail up the hill and continue through the circuit; the path is easily followed throughout. Come back to the parking spot and if you like, take the spur trail to the river.

You should have no difficulty following the fire-road trail. To complete the circuit you must walk a short distance on Poplar Hill Road, passing a few homes and the old Poplar Grove Methodist Church and cemetery. This is a pretty stretch of narrow road, with comparatively little traffic. Be sure to walk on the left side, facing oncoming traffic.

Hike 9.8 Phoenix Circuit

Moderate 2.5-mile woodland and river trail; good for bird-watching.

Trail's Attractions

The entire length of Phoenix Circuit overlooks Gunpowder Falls; the woodland trail runs above the river, and the abandoned railroad track bed passes beside it. Close to the river, you will hear the sounds of frogs and of the many birds who live in the lush growth along the water.

Open and sunny as it follows the railroad bed, the trail is shady as it travels high above the west bank of the Gunpowder, through the mountain laurel, tulip poplar, and white pine woods. All the common spring and summer wildflowers are abundant in this area. From the west side of the loop, you can look across the river to the remains of the small, old settlement of Phoenix, once a thriving cotton duck mill town.

Unpleasant features of this trail include the illegal use of motorcycles, trash dumping, and illegal target shooting and hunting. Solutions to these problems will be found only when the public, in sufficient numbers, expresses its concern to the Bureau of Engineering and to the county government.

Directions

From Beltway Exit 24, take I 83 north about 5.5 miles, to the Shawan Road exit. Drive east on Shawan Road about a mile, until it dead-ends on Old York Road. Turn right on Old York Road and head south about a quarter of a mile, to Ashland Road. Turn left and drive on Ashland Road about half a mile, to a fork in the road. Take the left fork, Paper Mill Road, and drive about 1.7 miles (passing over Gunpowder Falls) to the intersection with Phoenix Road. Turn left onto Phoenix Road and travel about 1 mile to the cinder parking area on the left side of the road (opposite Carroll Road and the pond).

The hike begins on a wide path alongside the abandoned railroad bed on the banks of Gunpowder Falls. Hike downstream toward the railroad bridge. Before crossing the bridge you may wish to climb the steep hillside on your left, up to the spur road from Phoenix Road, for a fine view in all directions. Return to the railroad bed and cross the bridge. Immediately after crossing, pick up a footpath that leads back upstream. After following it for a short distance, climb the steep slope to your left (there is no trail for this short stretch) to the rocky pinnacle that you will see from the footpath. In warm summer months watch out for copperheads on the rocks. From the pinnacle, follow the dirt fire road north through the woods to the bridge. Cross the bridge and walk back along the river and the railroad tracks to the entrance.

Hike 9.9 Glen Ellen

Excellent, varied, moderate 5-mile (one way) hike with many small circuits and shorter hikes possible; recommended in all seasons.

Trail's Attractions

"Glen Ellen" was the name of an estate that once occupied the surrounding land; ruins of Glen Ellen mansion lie just offshore. The trail offers a lot to both the casual hiker and the dedicated naturalist. It is in generally good condition, which makes even the eastern section relatively easy to traverse. The area is varied enough to interest the beginner in both winter and warm weather tromps. Many hikers will want to devote a day each to the eastern and western sections of the trail.

Attractions of the area include tall second-growth deciduous woods, on the slopes beside Rush Brook, and a varied understory. For a good wildflower walk, take the loop and bushwhack to the sandy beach—a fine place for lunch or for peaceful contemplation of the lake. The bushwhack to the beach is rugged and involves clambering along, and sometimes in, a small trickle of a stream, but it is worth the effort.

From the center section of the trail, several footpaths and fire-road trails lead through dogwoods and pines to the water's edge. The field of young planted pines that slopes down to the lake in this area is a good place from which to watch the migrating waterfowl that rest offshore, without disturbing them. Unfortunately, the view from this field will be obstructed when the pines planted there grow larger. If you are careful you may also observe, at close hand, ducks feeding in the many small coves nearby. Wading birds such as the snowy egret also feed in the marshy, deeply indented mouth of the stream just east of Hampton Cove. Those who feel that areas such as small marshes should be preserved for a well-balanced area environment ought to encourage the bureau to refrain from planting right up to and in the marshes and to leave an occasional field in its natural state.

Near the trail entrance on Seminary Avenue, many obscure paths lead into the forest of tall white pines. If you follow any one of these for a short distance you will soon realize that it is an animal path. As the path becomes narrower, animal droppings become more numerous, and you will have to stoop lower to avoid tree limbs and brush. Observing the footprints and droppings found on an animal path is a good way for the novice to sense the presence of the shyer

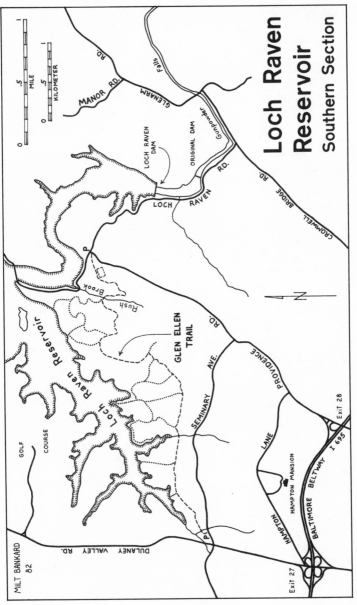

Loch Raven Reservoir
Southern Section

MANOR RD.

GLENARM
Falls

LOCH RAVEN DAM

ORIGINAL DAM

Gunpowder

LOCH RAVEN RD.

CROMWELL BRIDGE RD.

Rush Brook

Loch Raven Reservoir

GOLF COURSE

DULANEY VALLEY RD.

GLEN ELLEN TRAIL

SEMINARY AVE.

PROVIDENCE RD.

HAMPTON LANE

HAMPTON MANSION

BALTIMORE BELTWAY I 695

Exit 27

Exit 28

N

MILT BANKARD 82

USGS Towson

MILE

KILOMETER

forest animals. This can be especially rewarding in snowy weather; but once you become familiar with the tracks left by the two sharp pointed pads of the deer's hoof, for example, you will begin to spot them everywhere on watershed trails.

Directions

Begin at either end of Glen Ellen Trail. To reach the westernmost end, take Dulaney Valley Road north from Beltway Exit 27 for about .8 mile, to Seminary Avenue (at the first traffic signal). Turn right onto Seminary Avenue and park on the left shoulder, a few hundred yards down the road, on the near side of a small bridge over a stream. The trail begins as a dirt fire road. Somewhat littered at first, it soon becomes more sightly.

To reach the eastern end of the trail, take Beltway Exit 28 and drive north on Providence Road 2.7 miles, to its end at Loch Raven Road. Park at the intersection; on the far side of the road is a pull-out with room for five or more cars. The trail entrance is on the southwest corner of the intersection and is marked by a wooden gate bearing a No Trespassing sign. About three hundred yards from the entrance is an abandoned sawmill, and nearby, some dumped trash. Continue into the woods, where the trail becomes more pleasing.

Short and long hikes can be arranged on the Glen Ellen Trail by imaginatively combining the many small circuits available. A short hike begun from the Providence Road entrance would lead for the most part through shaded woodlands, except for the fine views and beach by the Glen Ellen ruins, whereas a hike from the Seminary Avenue entrance would take you through more open areas, allowing you to explore more shoreline and observe more waterfowl.

Hike 9.10 Laurel Woodlands

Easy, gently hilly 2.4-mile (one-way) and 2.5-mile (circuit) hikes; especially fine wildflower trail; recommended in all seasons.

Trail's Attractions

The natural attractions of the land through which the Laurel Woodlands Trail passes are so varied and unusual that the area has been proposed for designation as a special nature preserve. Part of the woodland is in very tall trees, mainly tulip poplars and oaks, with occasional sweet gum, sour gum, and hickory trees. The area has been carefully and selectively logged in the past, so timber self-reproduction is optimal; there are trees of at least four distinct age groups throughout the stand.

The Laurel Woodlands area has a remarkable diversity of terrain, which provides a variety of habitats for plants and animals. A stream with a luxuriant growth of ferns and wildflowers courses down one rocky declivity. Here you may hear the veery and the Louisiana waterthrush singing. In one thin woods is a scattering of redbud trees. The hooded warbler and the ovenbird nest in nearby denser woodlands. Steep slopes of mountain laurel under contorted chestnut oaks provide extraordinary views of the forest canopy and of the lake. The area, full of numerous common and rare wildflowers, is of great botanical interest. If you are fortunate enough to observe a rare bloom, you have, of course, an obligation to leave it for the next fortunate observer to see.

There are many possible short circuit hikes for naturalists of all kinds, as well as a 5-mile (round trip) shaded trip for hikers interested primarily in woodland exercise. Quite a few of these trails could be confusing, but the area is small enough that you should soon be able to reorient yourself.

Directions

No parking is permitted along Morgan Mill Road near Loch Raven Road, and parking is limited along Loch Raven Road, so the following directions lead you to the trail entrance on Morgan Mill Road, near Manor Road. From Beltway Exit 28, drive north on Providence Road 2.7 miles to Loch Raven Road. Turn left on Loch Raven Road and drive approximately 1.5 miles to Morgan Mill Road, which is a short distance beyond the bridge over Loch Raven Reservoir. Turn right onto Morgan Mill Road and drive half a mile to a wide dirt pull-out on the right, just beyond a small, unmarked

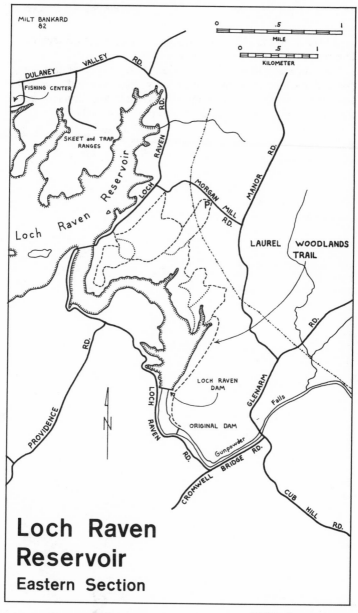

MILT BANKARD
82

DULANEY VALLEY RD.

FISHING CENTER

SKEET and TRAP
RANGES

Loch Raven Reservoir

Loch Raven

LOCH RAVEN RD.

MORGAN MILL RD.

PT.

MANOR RD.

LAUREL WOODLANDS TRAIL

PROVIDENCE RD.

LOCH RAVEN RD.

LOCH RAVEN DAM

ORIGINAL DAM

GLENARM

Falls

RD.

Gunpowder

CROMWELL BRIDGE RD.

CUB HILL RD.

N

0   .5   1
MILE

0   .5   1
KILOMETER

Loch Raven
Reservoir
Eastern Section

road leading to the left. There is room to park ten to fifteen cars. The trail entrance is marked by two posts and a wire.

You can make several short and medium-length circuits using this trail; the hike to the dam is especially interesting and scenic. Do not attempt to climb on the dam. It is possible to continue beyond the dam, through a nice meadow, to the original dam.

10. Lake Roland–
Robert E. Lee Park

Baltimore City's Robert E. Lee Park, or Lake Roland, as it is commonly called, means many things to many people. It is a city park for picnicking, daytime or evening strolls, boating, fishing, and ice skating in the winter. It is also a fine place for hiking and nature study. The park includes a marsh, deciduous woods, a serpentine barrens, many springs, streams, and a river. You can see birds, from great blue herons to starlings; plants, from orchids to dandelions; and trees, from blackjack oak to tulip poplar. In all, ten different wildlife habitats are said to be represented in the park.

Most people know only the section of the park near the lake, by the dam. In this area are picnic tables, open and grassy playing fields, some popular fishing spots, and footpaths at the lake's edge. You can rent rowboats, in season, near the parking lot above the dam. A section of ice near a pavilion above the dam is cleared of snow when the ice is safe for skating. At such times a safety patrol is always present.

Fewer people are familiar with the more remote parts of the park, north of the lake along the Jones Falls—the hilly pine barrens and the marsh. These areas are fairly isolated from the sights and sounds of the city. Although the park lands are not extensive, there are areas of beauty and serenity remarkable because they have been preserved so close to the heart of the city.

Urban Park Problems

Lake Roland is basically a fine park, unspoiled and wilder than most urban parks. Careless trash dumping, pollution of the park's streams and lake, and siltation in the lake, however, are causes for concern. A local conservationist is working to focus public attention on the park's problems. If you enjoy the park, contact a local conservation organization to volunteer your services and write to the city expressing your support for Lake Roland's protection and improvement.

Lake Roland Marsh in winter (Bob Wirth)

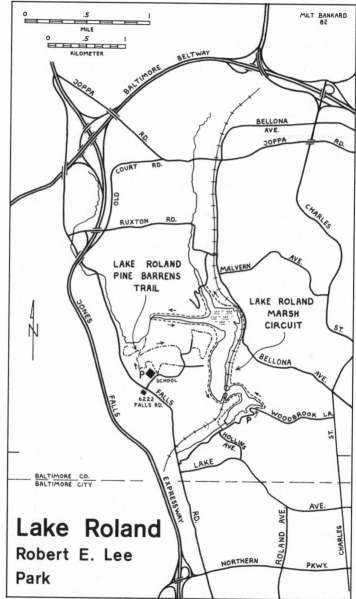

MILT BANKARD
82

Cockeysville USGS Baltimore West

BALTIMORE CO.
BALTIMORE CITY

Lake Roland

Robert E. Lee

Park

119

Hike 10.1 Lake Roland Marsh Circuit

Easy, exciting 4-mile circuit around the marsh; shorter hikes possible; recommended in all seasons.

Trail's Attractions

Baltimoreans are privileged to have the Lake Roland Marsh so close at hand for study and enjoyment. Conservationists trying to construct a marsh in Connecticut consider Lake Roland Marsh priceless. The Lake Roland Marsh Circuit takes you completely around the marsh, affording vantage points from many angles and often providing concealment from the marsh's inhabitants. At the north end, near Roland Run, you can walk into a grassy, boggy section. On the eastern side, near Towson Run, is a point from which you can see the whole lake and marsh in the distance. The peninsula on the western shore has a path that is bordered on the lake side by low bushes. If you conceal yourself in these bushes, you can watch ducks and wading birds nearby without disturbing them.

In the marsh area you will see wading birds, pond ducks, migrating waterfowl, hawks, and stream valley warblers, as well as birds of the woods' edge. In addition to common spring and summer wildflowers along stream banks and paths, marsh flowers such as the delicate blue and yellow wild iris grow here. This trail will be exciting for naturalists of all degrees of experience.

Along the trail, in addition to the flowers, you will encounter automobile tires, plastic bleach bottles, and beer cans. In addition to working to redirect the system that condones such waste, you can help improve the immediate situation by joining in the periodic Lake Roland cleanups, led by conservation groups, and by indicating your concern to the Baltimore City Park Board.

To beat the crowds of fishermen and picnickers in spring and early summer, marsh watchers should arrive either early in the morning or late in the afternoon.

Directions

To reach the parking lot at Lake Roland and the suggested beginning of the hike, approach the area via Charles Street or Falls

Road. From Charles Street turn west onto Lake Avenue. Follow Lake Avenue about .9 mile to Hollins Lane. Turn right and follow Hollins Lane to its end at the park, where you turn right to reach the parking lot. From Falls Road, turn onto the park road at the Robert E. Lee Park sign, just past Mount Washington and before the bridge over the Jones Falls. Follow the road to its end at the parking lot. In summer, when the park is crowded, it may be easier to park near the lake along Bellona Avenue, where there is ample parking space.

Begin Lake Roland Marsh Circuit by circling east (counter-clockwise) from the farthest parking area, just above the dam. This trail offers the best view of the entire lake and marsh and will allow you to see the area through which you will hike. Hike around the lower portion of the lake, southeast of the railroad bridge. At first, you can follow either the wide bed of the former through-road (Woodbrook Lane) or the fishermen's path along the shore. (Fishing for bass or catfish can be rewarding here.) Soon the trail turns away from the paved entrance to Woodbrook Lane and leads to the marsh. Be prepared for occasional climbs over or under large logs.

When the trail meets the railroad tracks, it turns right to follow them. There is a wide path beside the tracks; be careful—this railroad is in use. You can use paths along the shore on this stretch too, but be careful of poison ivy in summer. The remainder of the trail consists principally of footpaths, except for the portion along the west side of the lake. Here you may also follow the bed of an abandoned railroad, whose rails have been taken up in places. At the south end of the lake, the trail again follows the bed of an abandoned railroad; it soon crosses railroad tracks that are very much in use and leads back to the dam.

At the north end of the lake, the trail turns northwest (away from the railroad tracks) and enters the woods. This entrance may be hidden by thick vegetation during the summer months. To avoid this problem, you may wish to forego the better views and hike in a clockwise direction, following the trail up the west side of the lake. The trail changes from wide to narrow and back occasionally; it is sometimes elevated, affording good views of the lake.

You can make a quick late-afternoon or early morning visit to the marsh from the point where Roland Run (at the north end of the lake) crosses under Ruxton Circle.

Hike 10.2 Lake Roland Pine Barrens

Easy 2-mile circuit (plus side trails) with unusual ecological features; recommended in all seasons; see chapter 5 (Soldiers' Delight) for a description of a similar but much larger area that is more remote from the city of Baltimore.

Trail's Attractions

The pine barrens at Lake Roland is probably the only such barrens in America existing within the limits of a major urban area. It is characterized by serpentine rock closely underlying the surface, scattered pines, blackjack oaks, and large open and grassy areas. The area is especially beautiful in autumn, winter, and early spring, when the muted colors of the grasses and the green of the pines stand out best. The many springs originating in the rocky area near the trail entrance produce fern-lined boggy places and tiny streams. Beyond the pine barrens, the trail extends through deciduous woods to the Jones Falls Valley and the marsh. You can easily arrange short circuit hikes. Thoughtlessly dumped trash makes the trail unsightly in places, but if hikers will aid in cleaning up the area, the trash need not be a permanent feature of the landscape.

Directions

To reach the trail entrance, take Falls Road and turn on an unmarked road about three quarters of a mile north of Lake Avenue (just north of Mount Washington). The unmarked road is on the right-hand side of Falls Road, across from the house whose number is 6222. It leads to a small school building, several private homes, and the park.

There is space for many cars in the school parking lot at all hours, except when school is in session. Beyond the parking lot, the paved road leads to the park entrance and private homes.

The trail is a combination of footpaths, roads, and an abandoned railroad bed. You can make a circuit hike by following all the outermost trails in the area, passing first through the pine barrens, then down to the deciduous woods along Jones Falls Valley and the marsh. It is possible to make a circuit of the marsh also, although the Pine Barrens hike alone contains enough interesting features to lure the hiker back many times in different seasons throughout the year.

11. Patapsco State Park

Introduction to the Area

Patapsco Valley State Park is situated on the western fringe of Baltimore. Extending from Sykesville and Liberty Reservoir in the north to Elkridge in the southeast, it encompasses over 20 miles of the Patapsco River and its surrounding ridges and provides an excellent, nearby opportunity to enjoy the out-of-doors. In addition to providing habitat for diverse plants and animals, this 15,000-acre preserve offers picnicking, camping, hiking, fishing, canoeing, horseback riding, and if you dare, swimming.

The park contains six developed areas: McKeldin, in the fork of the north and south branches of the river; Pickall, on the east bank, south of Johnnycake Road; Hollofield, on the west side of the river, south of U.S. 40; Hilton Avenue, at the end of Hilton Avenue in Catonsville; Glen Artney/Avalon, near Relay, accessible from U.S. 1; and Orange Grove, on the west bank, reached through the Avalon area.

The park sponsors diverse outdoor activities at numerous different times and locations throughout the area. Picnicking pavilions may be reserved in all the developed areas, and there are family campgrounds in the Hilton and Hollofield areas. There are also over 15 miles of marked trails and many more of unmarked paths. For more information, contact the park headquarters at 1100 Hilton Avenue, Baltimore, Maryland 21228 or telephone (301)747–6602.

Please note that in the developed areas, there is an entrance fee (currently $3 per car) charged on weekends, from mid-April through Labor Day.

Hiking

Within the park, the Patapsco River flows generally from the northwest to the southeast. The exception is the south branch, which flows due east from Sykesville to join the main current. Orient your map to determine the river's exact direction. The

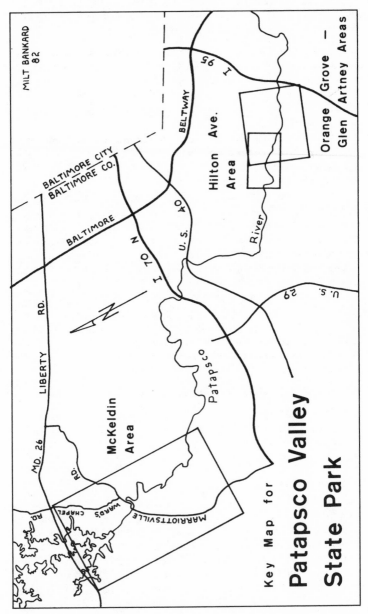

Key Map for **Patapsco Valley State Park**

MILT BANKARD 82

BALTIMORE CITY / BALTIMORE CO.

BALTIMORE

BELTWAY

I 95

Hilton Ave. Area

Orange Grove — Glen Artney Areas

River

U.S. 40

I 70 N

U.S. 29

Patapsco

LIBERTY RD.

MD. 26

McKeldin Area

WARD'S CHAPEL RD.

MARRIOTTSVILLE

N

park's average width is only half a mile, so although an area may seem wild, you will never be far from a residential or commercial community. To avoid getting lost, check your map before you start, and when hiking, pay attention to man-made structures, such as power-line crossings, as well as to significant topographical and geological features.

Use caution when crossing the railroad right-of-way, which runs the full length of the park. Do not use the tracks as a trail, and please stay out of tunnels. Be aware that debris thrown up by a passing train can injure your eyes.

Over the centuries, the Patapsco River and its feeder streams have cut deep channels into the surrounding hills. As a result, there are many lovely but potentially dangerous overlooks in the park, and many of the trails offer conditions similar to those found in the mountains of western Maryland. Unless you are bushwhacking, please stay on the trails. Do not cut across switchbacks. Erosion is a constant problem on these steep trails.

The trail directions that follow include both marked and un-marked paths. As an aid to hikers, descriptions of significant turns are accompanied by compass readings, in parentheses, which indicate the direction to be taken.

Take only pictures; leave only footprints. Enjoy.

Hike 11.1 Patapsco Branch Circuit

Easy 3.5-mile circuit with a 100-foot elevation change and three steep climbs; located in the McKeldin area.

Trail's Attractions

The McKeldin area boasts several short trails that are ideal for novice hikers and for children. The Patapsco Branch Circuit is the longest of these. You may hike shorter segments of this circuit by using connecting trails, not shown on the accompanying map, which lead to the developed area of the park.

For most of its length, the trail follows the river—first the south branch and then the north branch. It is well maintained and mostly level, the most difficult climb occurring near the end of the hike, where the trail makes use of a switchback to gain the ridge.

This short trail provides an excellent opportunity for plant and bird identification; be sure to bring along guidebooks. Wild azalea, May-apple, spiderwort, wild ginger, columbine, spenulose wood fern, and cinnamon fern are among the many plants found along the trail. You may also encounter bluebirds, salamanders, beavers, ducks, and hawks. Through each season the trail offers a changing panorama.

Directions

From the Beltway (I 695) take Exit 16 west onto I 70. Continue west for 8.5 miles to Exit 81 and turn north onto Marriottsville Road. After 3.4 miles park on the left, between the river and the railroad. If you prefer to leave your car in the developed area of the park, drive .7 mile north on Marriottsville Road to the entrance. Turn right and drive to the top of the hill. You can start the hike at the ranger station near the entrance.

From the Marriottsville Road parking area, hike .3 mile north on Marriottsville Road, watching carefully for traffic, to a petroleum pipe-line crossing and turn right (approximately 160°). A few yards into the woods, the trail drifts left to intersect a dirt road at the base of a high hill. Follow this road out onto the flood plain by the river.

Turn right (140°) at the intersection onto a yellow-marked park trail along the flood plain. At the next trail junction turn right again. The trail will climb along a bank above the river. Eventually it climbs to the picnic area on top of the hill where it intersects a paved road (with restrooms on the right). Here you have two choices: hike straight ahead on the marked trail—the easier course—or turn onto the road. To reach the waterfall, turn right onto this road. A well-worn trail at the end of the road descends to the waterfall. This is a lovely spot for a lunch stop.

Turn left along the river and pass several connecting trails that climb to your left. The trail crosses the face of a large sloping rock, which can be slippery when wet. In the spring, a profusion of wildflowers fills this area. Poison ivy is also abundant.

Three counties come together at the confluence of the north and south branches of the Patapsco River. You are hiking in Carroll County, but to your left, across the north branch, is Baltimore County and to your right, across the south branch, is Howard

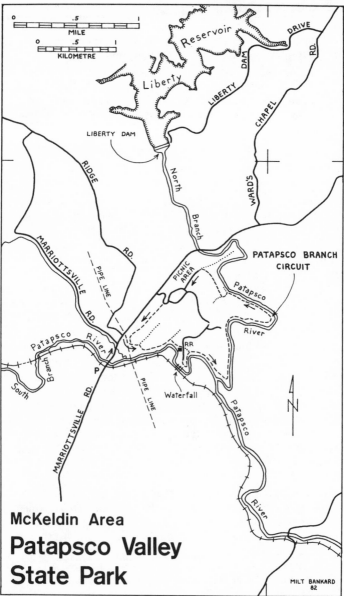

PATAPSCO BRANCH
CIRCUIT

McKeldin Area
**Patapsco Valley
State Park**

MILT BANKARD
82

County. A few yards upriver there are stepping stones across the north branch. When the river is low, the adventurous hiker can cross to the other bank and explore. This hike, however, continues along the west bank.

As you hike upriver, note the large limestone boulders on your left. They mark the edge of a veritable fern garden; from here to the limestone cliff farther upriver, the forest floor is covered with ferns.

The trail turns abruptly to the left (220°) and climbs steeply, with a switchback, to the ridge top. You can easily miss this turn, but you will soon realize it if you do, because the trail ahead ends in a few yards at the base of a limestone cliff.

At the trail fork, turn right, passing along the northeast face of the ridge, and cross a ravine. At the next junction, turn left and climb to the picnic area and a paved road. During the winter there is a fine view of Liberty Dam from the end of this road. Turn left on the paved road and continue along the ridge to the ranger station at the park entrance.

From the ranger station, hike down the entrance road to the first curve. Turn left onto a wide, obvious trail leading into the woods. Note the flagstone along this section of the trail. Flagstone quarries still operate in and around Marriottsville. If you started this hike in the developed area of the park, turn left at the base of the hill; otherwise, return to your car via the pipe-line and Marriottsville Road.

Hike 11.2 Sawmill Branch–Buzzard Rock Circuit

Moderate, two and three-quarter-mile hike with a 240-foot elevation change, several stream crossings, and at least one steep climb; located in the Hilton Avenue area.

Trail's Attractions

This hike begins and ends in the developed section of the Hilton area. It encompasses two park-designated trails—the Sawmill Branch Circuit (blazed in red) and the Buzzard Rock Trail (blazed in yellow). Together these trails provide access to the woods and the stream valley south and west of the campground.

Pig Run waterfall along Saw Mill Branch Trail (Jay Mittenthal)

Rocky Sawmill Branch and Pig Run abound with tumbling waterfalls. Common spring and summer wildflowers can be found throughout the area, and numerous varieties of fern inhabit the stream bank. All the native woodland birds frequent the area, and you can see meadow-preferring species in the power-line area. Deer and other creatures also share this habitat, and although you may not see them, they often leave their tracks along the stream. In the evening, buzzards roost in the trees near Buzzard Rock.

Directions

Take Beltway Exit 13 to Frederick Road and turn west to pass through the community of Catonsville. After traveling 1.2 miles from the Beltway, turn left onto Rolling Road. There is a traffic light at this intersection, and Hillcrest Elementary School will be on your right. Proceed .2 mile to a fork in the road and stay right onto Hilton Avenue. The park entrance is on your right 1.5 miles from the fork. After entering the park, take the first possible right, onto the family campground road. Park under the power lines, preferably away from the picnic pavilion.

After parking, hike a few yards up the campground road to the beginning of the Sawmill Branch Trail. The trail entrance is identified by a sign. Turn left (310°) and hike downhill, parallel to the power lines. About one hundred yards from the campground road, turn right (5°) at a fork, onto a less-obvious trail.

This trail parallels the left fork for a few yards before diverging to descend to a bog at the head of Pig Run. Cross the bog in a north-northwesterly direction. This section of the trail can be obscure in places, so watch carefully. At the far edge of the bog, turn to 240° and climb. Turn right (330°) at the first trail junction, onto the Buzzard Rock Trail. If you reach the power-line cut, you have gone too far. After turning, climb to the top of the ridge and continue in a northerly direction. Note the collapsed stone fence, a remnant of the area's agricultural past. Wild ginger and a few rare wildflowers grow in this area.

Cross the campground road (15°) and continue through the woods to a trail junction, where you will turn left (240°) onto an old dirt road. The road narrows to a trail and gradually descends as it skirts the north side of the campground. You will pass several

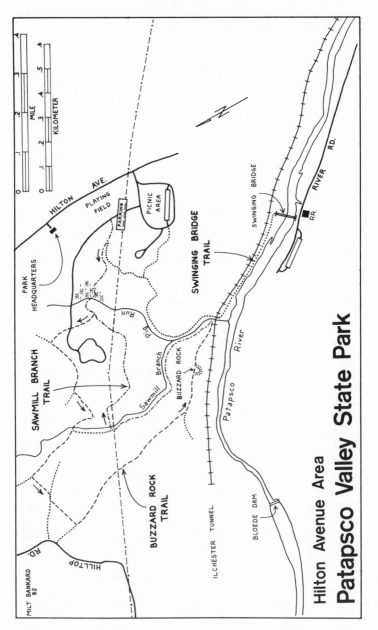

Hilton Avenue Area

Patapsco Valley State Park

camping pads and connecting trails on your left. Swing gradually to the north and begin a steeper descent, turn sharply left (255°) at a large fallen log, and continue along the side of the hill. This trail will descend in a north-northwesterly direction, on a switchback, to Sawmill Branch.

Cross the branch and climb steeply uphill at 300°. Swing to 20° and continue to climb the ridge, which has a steep bank down on both sides. A few yards south of the crest of the hill, turn left (270°) onto another trail. This turn is easily missed. If you cross the top of the hill, you have gone too far. The correct path meanders in a westerly direction, across a relatively flat area.

At the next trail junction, turn right (355°), walk about twenty yards, and turn left (265°) on an obscure trail. Cross a flat wooded expanse (beware of brambles) and an old dirt track. This area was once the Hilltop Archery Range; Hilltop Road is just out of sight to your right.

The trail will end at a dirt road. Turn left (170°) and follow this road under the power lines and into the woods. It will swing left (150°) along the ridge above the river. The road remains wide and obvious all the way to Buzzard Rock, which is on the right, a few feet below the ridge. From this overlook you can see upriver beyond Bloede's Dam (ca. 1907). It is a lovely view in all seasons of the year. Scan the trees while you are here; buzzards often roost near the rocks.

South of the rocks, the road narrows to a trail and clings to the ridge crest as it descends toward Sawmill Branch. Sections of this trail are steep and tend to crumble, thus providing hazardous footing.

At the railroad grade turn left (20°), above Sawmill Branch, and hike upstream. The path will continue to descend along the stream bank until you reach a connecting trail that fords the branch. You can either cross the branch, turn north upstream, and walk east along Pig Run to complete the hike or, for a more scenic trip, with an accent on stream bed attractions, continue upstream along the bank of Sawmill Branch. You can extend this hike by crossing the branch here, hiking downstream under the railroad bridge, and walking southeast down the Patapsco River to the swinging bridge. See the descriptions of Hikes 11.3 and 11.4 for directions.

A short distance upstream along Sawmill Branch, you will see a lovely waterfall. Beyond the falls, the trail switches from bank to bank, staying on the flood plain as much as possible.

At the power-line cut, a cross trail descends steeply from the left, fords the branch, and climbs the opposite hill. Turn right (110°) on this trail, cross the branch, and climb up the power-line cut. A short distance up the hill, the trail turns sharply to the right (180°) and enters the woods. Instead of scrambling to the top of the hill, follow the trail as it circles gradually higher along the western and southern slopes. During the winter there is a lovely view of the Sawmill Branch Valley from this trail.

Cross the power-line cut (70°) just below a tower. To the southeast you have a panoramic view across Pig Run. The opposite hill is gorgeous when the meadow flowers are in bloom. Shortly after reentering the woods, the trail swings to the right and descends. Pass the junction where, earlier, you turned onto Buzzard Rock Trail and retrace your steps down to the bog and the parking area.

Hike 11.3 Vineland–Cascade Run Shuttle

Moderate, 5-mile hike, with a 280-foot elevation change and three steep climbs; located in Glen Artney and Orange Grove sections. This hike requires a car shuttle (a vehicle parked at each end). The parking areas and entrance trails also provide access to alternate hikes.

Trail's Attractions

About two-thirds of the hike is on equestrian trails. Exercise caution when you encounter horses.

The trail bisects the lower section of the park, from Rolling Road on the east to Landing Road on the west. It passes through Glen Artney, skirts the Hilton Avenue area, and crosses through Orange Grove. Along the way you will be treated to wooded stream valleys, a meadow in the first stages of reforestation, a swinging bridge, a hemlock-lined gorge, and a tumbling falls. Wildflowers abound in season and myriad birds and animals frequent the more isolated areas of the trail.

Directions

From the Beltway take Exit 12 west on Wilkens Avenue. Wilkens Avenue will end at Rolling Road (1.5 miles). Turn left and drive .6 mile. Park on the right shoulder, opposite a turnoff to Md. 166. A few yards south of the turnoff, a dirt road leads to the right (240°) into a meadow. This is the Vineland Trail.

To shuttle a vehicle to Landing Road, take Md. 166 south 2.3 miles to U.S. 1. Turn right (southwest) and proceed 1.5 miles to Montgomery Road (traffic light). Make a second right. At 1.3 miles turn right again onto Landing Road. Continue on Landing Road for 1.5 miles. Just .3 mile north of the Trinity School entrance, park on your left, in a wooded glen. There is parking here for about five cars. The trail enters the woods on the opposite (east) side of the road. Start here and do the hike in reverse, or leave a vehicle here and return to Rolling Road.

From Rolling Road, hike west along the south edge of the meadow, then follow the clearly defined road as it descends steeply to the stream valley. Continue southwest, downstream, along Soapstone Branch. This is a very pleasant area; set between the hills, with a murmuring brook and an avian chorus, it is a world apart. Most of the common spring and summer wildflowers grow here, and ferns are well established along the stream bank. The forest in this area is predominantly beech.

There are several stone outcrops in the stream bed. Particularly noticeable at the fourth and fifth stream crossings, these outcrops consist of metamorphic rocks, over 500 million years old. They originated as lava that was buried under subsequent deposits, where heat and pressure changed them into their present form. Then, about 400 million years ago, this area rose, and over the next 150 million years, the younger deposits eroded away. About 10 million years ago, the Patapsco River began to cut its present channel. Over the centuries the bedrock has been exposed and worn away; today, it is visible throughout the park.

At the power-line crossing the trail makes an obvious right to ford the stream. Once across, you have three choices. First, you may turn right, pass an access road up to the power-line cut, and follow an equestrian trail upstream (50°). A steep switchback

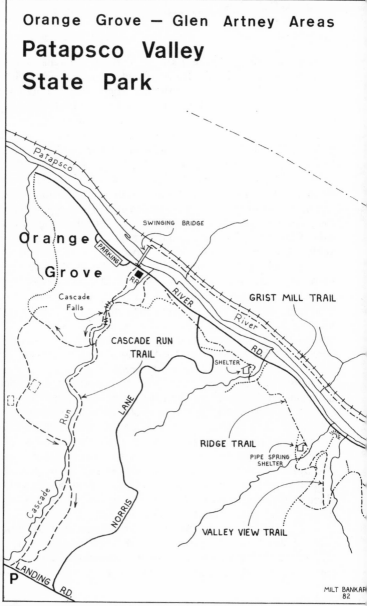

Orange Grove — Glen Artney Areas

Patapsco Valley
State Park

Patapsco

SWINGING BRIDGE

Orange

Grove

PARKING

RD.

Cascade
Falls

RIVER

River

GRIST MILL TRAIL

CASCADE RUN
TRAIL

RD.

SHELTER

Run

LANE

RIDGE TRAIL

PIPE SPRING
SHELTER

Cascade

NORRIS

VALLEY VIEW TRAIL

P

LANDING
RD.

MILT BANKAR
82

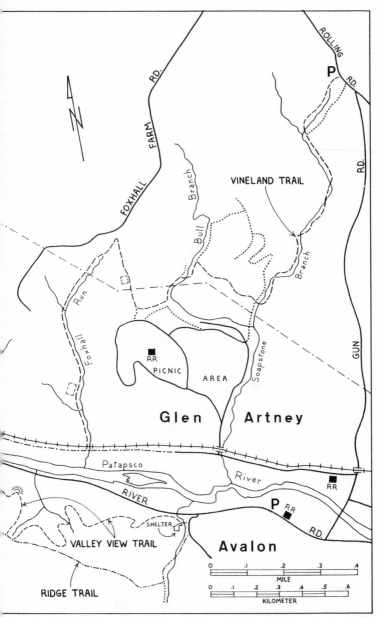

ROLLING RD.

P

FOXHALL FARM RD.

VINELAND TRAIL

Bull Branch

Branch

GUN RD.

Foxhall Run

Soapstone

RR
PICNIC AREA

Glen   Artney

Patapsco   River

RR

P RR

RIVER   RD.

SHELTER

VALLEY VIEW TRAIL

Avalon

RIDGE TRAIL

| 0 | .1 | .2 | .3 | .4 |
MILE

| 0 | .1 | .2 | .3 | .4 | .5 | .6 |
KILOMETER

climbs through a mature forest almost to the top of the ridge. Then the trail swings to the northeast along the slope and climbs, while circling to the northwest. At the trail junction on top of the ridge, turn right (355°) and continue north to the next trail fork. Turn left (250°) and go down a wash to Bull Branch. (The right fork ends at a gate to a meadow.) Follow the branch (200°) downstream to a crossing. Ford the stream, cross the flood plain, and climb to an abandoned road. Turn left and follow this trace as it swings south. After crossing a wash, turn right (205°) onto a trail that climbs steeply to a meadow. If you reach a chasm you have gone too far on the road. Continue across the meadow (300°) to a well-worn path and turn right (5°) to climb to the top of Cistern Hill.

Second, for a shorter hike, climb to the power-line cut and hike north along its eastern edge, skirting a ravine. The power-line cut is full of poison ivy, so be careful. Just over the second hill, leave the cut and bushwhack to the right until you reach a wash. Turn left and descend to Bull Branch. At the stream turn left (225°) on the equestrian trail and hike downstream to the ford. From this point on, follow the directions given above.

For the third alternative, turn left (205°) and continue down-stream to the junction of Bull Branch and Soapstone Branch. Cross the stream into the Glen Artney picnic area and continue at 240° to a gravel road. Climb steeply and pass a connecting road to the left. The gravel road will continue to climb along the edge of the ridge, providing an excellent view of the valley to your right. Eventually it will swing to 285° and become fairly flat.

At a fork, turn right (315°) on an abandoned road. For a short distance, the gravel road will parallel this road while continuing to climb toward the ridge top. The abandoned road continues along the side of the ridge until it reaches a chasm, where it turns left and climbs steeply. At the paved road turn right (320°). Be careful of traffic on this road. When you see a fence on your right, turn right on the well-used path (5°) that leads to the top of Cistern Hill.

From the top you will have a panoramic view of the meadow and adjacent lands to the north. Since this property became a part of the park it has been allowed to reforest at a natural pace. The brick tower is a cistern constructed over one hundred years ago. Its exact age is unknown, but a plat of the Foxhall farm, dated 1854, shows an unlabeled circle at this location. A hydraulic ram pumped water from Bull Branch to the cistern, thus providing running water to the main house and several tenant homes at a time when most people carried water from a well.

Descend toward the northern corner of the meadow (355°). At the meadow's edge, turn left (260°) on the meadow side of the hedgerow. You will see a maple with five trunks a few feet to the west. The trail passes to the right of this tree (255°) as it leaves the meadow and enters the hedgerow. Proceed down a wash to Foxhall Run. The Vineland Trail follows this stream (downstream) to the Patapsco River and the junction with the Grist Mill Trail. Along the way you will pass the concrete pylon foundation of a rental cabin once maintained by the park. A few yards farther downstream is the ruin of a stone building, believed to be a part of a mill that once operated on this creek.

At the railroad bridge, follow the stream under the bridge and turn right on the Grist Mill Trail, which is a closed-access road. As you hike along the river, take note of the flood plain to your left. In 1972 Hurricane Agnes inundated this area, sweeping away the existing plants and leaving behind a tank truck that is now a permanent part of the river scene. You may also want to study the construction of the railroad bridges. Most of these were built shortly after the Civil War, some without mortar.

By hiking a quarter of a mile straight upriver from the swinging bridge, you can reach the Sawmill Branch and the hiking trails in the Hilton area. For this hike, however, turn left and cross the bridge into the Orange Grove area. Here you may choose between the stream trail and the ridge trail. To follow the stream, swing left, around the restrooms, and follow the obvious trail up Cascade Run. Be prepared for stone hopping as you climb upstream.

To reach the Ridge Trail, continue straight up the steps, to the right of the restrooms. The trail climbs steeply under a hemlock canopy and then becomes level and crosses the run at a lovely pool below the upper falls.

The Ridge Trail joins the Cascade Run Trail at the upper falls. Continue upstream (205°) until you reach a fork in the trail. There are several large, flat-topped boulders between the trail and the stream. Turn right and pass between them to ford the run. After crossing, turn upstream.

At the next trail junction turn right (250°), along a feeder creek, to climb steeply to the top of the ridge. At the crest the trail swings north. Turn left (250°) at the top of the hill onto the Upper Cascade Run Trail. The bridle trail straight ahead returns to River Road near Bloede's Dam (see Hike 11.4).

The Upper Cascade Run Trail meanders south-southwest, touching two moderate ridges and passing a ruin. Eventually, it descends to Cascade Run. After crossing the stream, you should turn west, climb halfway up the ridge, and walk parallel to the run until you reach Landing Road.

Hike 11.4 Ridge-Valley View Trails

Moderate 3-mile hike (one way), with a 270-foot elevation change, several stream crossings, and as many steep climbs; located at Avalon and Orange Grove.

Trail's Attractions

The Ridge Trail extends from Avalon to Orange Grove along the southwestern ridge above the Patapsco River. It is wide and fairly obvious along much of its length. The Valley View Trail is a combination of two paths that loop from the Ridge Trail and a third path that extends from a pavilion at River Road, up the north face of the canyon, to the ridge top. It has fewer and more moderate grades as well as better views than corresponding sections of the Ridge Trail.

During the winter, portions of both trails afford excellent views of the valley below. In the spring, woodland wildflowers are common; native birds are abundant all year. From the road you may see wood ducks and mallards nesting along the river. Near Avalon, the roar of I 95 becomes somewhat annoying; the traffic sounds recede, however, as you descend from the ridge.

Directions

From the northbound lane of the Beltway, take Exit 10 to U.S. 1 south. From the southbound lane, take Exit 12A to Southwestern Boulevard and U.S. 1 south. Pass the Calvert Distillery and the Md. 166 interchange and turn right onto South Street (approximately 2.4 miles from the Beltway).

Thomas Viaduct in Patapsco State Park (Courtesy of the Baltimore County Chamber of Commerce)

Turn left onto the park entrance road immediately after turning right. This road will pass under the Thomas Viaduct, the world's oldest standing multiple-arched, stone railroad bridge. Farther along, on your right, is the Avalon Iron and Nail Works building. The town of Avalon was destroyed in the flood of 1868.

Turn left at the intersection, cross the river, and turn right on River Road. Continue until the road ends and park on the left in Orange Grove. The park headquarters were here until 1972, when Hurricane Agnes destroyed the building and most of the road, as far as Ilchester.

Start from the Orange Grove parking area. Hike northwest along River Road for about a quarter of a mile. This section of the road is closed to motor vehicles. At the trail junction turn left (210°), onto a bridle path, and climb steeply. At first a stream will parallel the trail on the right, but after a short distance, the path will swing left to take a south-southwesterly direction.

On top of the hill a trail will cross your path. Continue straight (190°) and descend to Cascade Run, where you will turn left (10°) to parallel the run. To your left, notice the stone ruins of privies. They are mute testimony to the development that once existed in this area of the park.

After a short distance the trail will cross the run (70°) to join a trail along the opposite bank. After crossing, turn downstream and hike about forty yards to Cascade Falls.

You may want to stop to explore this lovely falls, which is actually two cascades with a pool between. It is an ideal spot to have a snack or to rest and let the sound of rushing water wash away the cares of the world.

For a shorter trip, follow the trail from the pool, along the west bank, to the Orange Grove parking lot. Otherwise, return to the Ridge Trail at the top of the falls. Turn east (65°), hike around the face of the hill, and pass a boulder outcrop. A few yards beyond the boulders is a fork in the trail. Stay to the right (140°). Hereafter, unless told otherwise, disregard trails to the right; most lead out of the park, onto private property.

After descending almost to River Road, turn right (170°) on another trail and begin to climb. (The trail on the left continues down to River Road.) Within a short distance, you will intersect a dirt road (Norris Lane). Swing right (200°) and climb steeply. Turn left (150°) at the first possible trail or walk farther up the hill and turn left at the park boundary, where the road is blocked by a chain. The two trails soon merge; the combined trail descends to a stream and turns right (225°) to pass an old pavilion. After passing the shelter, it crosses the creek and turns downstream, leading to a gravel road. Turn right on the road (165°) and climb steeply. In the ravine to your left, near the top of the ridge, are the ruins of two more stone outhouses.

At the trail fork stay to the right (205°). The left fork descends to a shelter, while the right fork crosses a creek upstream from the pavilion. Note the pipe bringing spring water down to the shelter area. Check with a ranger before drinking from this or any other spring in the park.

After climbing a short distance, turn left (30°) onto the Valley View Trail, along the northwestern side of a ridge. Swing around the end of the ridge (200°) and take the narrow, flat trail along the eastern face. (Disregard a branch trail going down the hill and another path along the ridge top.) The trail leads in a southerly direction and eventually descends toward a stream.

At the trail junction, turn left (105°) on the Ridge Trail and descend along the stream. After fording the creek, begin to climb the next ridge. About 130 yards up the path, a branch trail will fork to the left (65°) to an overlook (good in winter only). Another forty-five yards up the hill, a second trail will branch left (120°). Turn here. This section of the Valley View Trail is lovely in all seasons; in winter it affords excellent views of the Patapsco River Valley. There is also a rock outcrop that makes an ideal lunch stop. The path eventually climbs (to the right of a ravine) back to the Ridge Trail.

Turn left (175°) on the Ridge Trail and cross the head of a wash. After a few feet, branch left (65°) onto the Valley View Trail and follow the south side of the ravine. Then swing right and continue level along the face of the hill. This trail makes a long, gradual descent to River Road. At the base of the hill, swing right, toward a pavilion. Cross the bridge over a stream and climb to a gravel driveway. This is the end of the first half of the hike. Here you may choose to return to your car via River Road (left) or via the Ridge Trail (right).

To avoid the traffic on River Road, turn right on the Ridge Trail and climb. After a few yards the gravel drive will swing left. Continue straight (215°) on a dirt road that parallels the stream. Eventually you will cross the stream on an old bridge and climb more steeply.

Make an abrupt right (330°) at the next trail junction. Pass two Valley View Trail junctions and stay on the ridge. By-pass an obvious trail which leads 195° to your left (not shown on the map) and follow the Ridge Trail as it swings north. It will descend, intersect the Valley View Trail again, and swing to the southwest to parallel a creek (on your right). After crossing the creek, begin to climb.

Pass the Valley View Trail once more and climb steeply. At the top of the hill, this path will join another trail. To your left is a bridle path that leads out of the park. Turn right (40°) and continue north. Near the end of the ridge begin a steep and obvious descent. Pass the last of the Valley View Trail junctions and continue on the Ridge Trail, retracing your steps to Cascade Falls. From the falls, follow the Cascade Run Trail downstream to the Orange Grove parking area.

12. Metropolitan Parks

Introduction to the Area

What Druid Hill, Cylburn, Leakin, and Gwynns Falls parks have in common is lack of interest on the part of the inhabitants of the metropolitan area. This neglect is occasioned in part by the public's ignorance of the parks' existence, which is due to a lack of publicity about their many attractions, and in part because of the city's failure to develop the parks fully as nature study centers and as scenic recreational resources. In addition to continuing their fine work at Cylburn, the city's conservationists and naturalists should focus their attention on the need for similar nature centers at the other high-potential city parks. Leakin Park's magnificent forests and Druid Hill Park's expanses have even greater potential than the Cylburn area.

Baltimore City's parks need an informed, interested, and vocal constituency. Citizens must encourage the city to carefully preserve its magnificent parks and to develop them properly. Leakin Park has been threatened by proposed expressway construction, the partitioning of Druid Hill Park is diminishing its attractiveness, and Cylburn is threatened by overdevelopment of the surrounding area. Call or write the Baltimore City Parks Department or the mayor to express your concern about the preservation of these parks. Read chapter 1 for information about ways in which citizens can influence city park policy.

Hike 12.1 Druid Hill Park

> Exceptionally good birding area at your doorstep; fine family hike, including a visit to the children's zoo; several-mile circuit hike possible; recommended in all seasons.

Trail's Attractions

In Druid Hill Park you will find a number of attractions—for families with children and for naturalists of all kinds and degrees of expertise. In addition to the main zoo, with its exhibits of exotic imported species, there is the children's zoo, in which children can approach and handle gentle animals. The city greenhouse, the conservatory, is free of charge and open to visitors all year round, seven days a week, 10:00 a.m. to 4:00 p.m.; it is especially enjoyable on rainy days. There are special flower exhibits in the fall, at Christmas, and at Easter. In the park, countless unusual species of tree have been planted for the enjoyment and mystification of amateur botanists. The entire park is a lovely picnic area, with plenty of open, grassy areas for impromptu games. One of the city's few public outdoor swimming pools is located here.

Druid Hill's natural attractions are outstanding. Druid Lake is on the waterfowl migration flyway, and amateur ornithologists have observed forty-six species of waterfowl on the lake, many of them migrating through but some wintering over. All three kinds of scoter, all the common ducks, old squaw, and a myriad of Canada geese have been observed here. A great blue heron has been seen feeding in the shallows, and herring and ringed-bill gulls, spotted sandpipers, and horned grebes pass through. It is a perfect spot to visit on a regular basis during migration and on days when you don't have enough time or the weather looks too foreboding to justify a long trip elsewhere. All three sister lakes are fairly good birding areas, too.

Inside the fenced-in zoo area, in addition to the captive animals on display and the children's zoo, are several natural attractions of great merit. The Baltimore Zoological Society maintains a native species duck breeding program in the duck pond. Besides the pinioned permanent residents, you will probably see black and mallard ducks and hooded mergansers wintering over, as well as many migrants. For novice ornithologists, the large duck pond and the small one adjacent to the island are good places to study ducks at close hand. In addition, there is enough cover around the duck pond to make it a good warbler migration stopover.

In the deep woods, along tiny streams below the children's zoo and behind the buffalo pens, is perhaps the best birding in the park; here you will find all the local year-round residents, including barred owls and great horned owls.

As the result of vandalism that included considerable harm to the zoo's animals, the zoo area of Druid Hill Park was fenced off in

1970. Entrance fees at the zoo are $1.50 for the general public, 50¢ for children aged two to eleven years, and $1.00 for senior citizens.

Hike 12.2 Cylburn Arboretum

Several short nature trails through an especially fine forest better suited for birding and botanizing than for high-speed hiking; year-round programs of nature activities, including guided walks and special children's programs.

Trail's Attractions

Cylburn's nature trails are short, intimate, and inviting. Along them you will find native trees, shrubs, and wildflowers, many of them labeled. There is a bog area directly in front of the mansion at the edge of the woods. Special plantings and feeding stations have attracted over one hundred species of birds to the arboretum. On the grounds many unusual shrubs, trees, and ground covers have been planted. The All American Selection Display Garden, the Formal Garden, the Herb Garden, and the Garden of the Senses are some of the main attractions. Cylburn is a good city spot to visit regularly to watch seasons change; its location makes it especially enjoyable for short walks at dusk or in early morning. Cylburn's footpaths are easily followed. There is a map on the front porch of the mansion and individual maps and self-guiding tours are available at the mansion office during working hours—weekdays 8:00 a.m. to 4:00 p.m. For information on scheduled guided walks and informative programs sponsored by the Cylburn Arboretum Association and other groups, call (301) 396–0180 or write Cylburn Mansion, Cylburn Arboretum, 4915 Greenspring Avenue, Baltimore, Maryland 21209.

Cylburn is a nature preserve, so you are not allowed to collect anything. In an effort to minimize man's impact on the natural scene, picnicking is also forbidden.

Baltimore City purchased Cylburn, an area of 176 acres, from the estate of Mrs. Bruce Cotton. The arboretum as we know it today was developed by the City Bureau of Recreation and Parks and citizens who formed the Cylburn Wildflower Preserve and Garden

A walk in a metropolitan park (Joe Sullivan)

Center, now known as the Cylburn Arboretum Association. The Victorian mansion, of Renaissance-revival style, has been preserved and now serves as arboretum headquarters. The mansion was built in 1861, using Maryland gneiss from the nearby Bare Hills region, and is of considerable architectural and decorative interest. It is used for group meetings on horticultural, ornithological, and conservational subjects.

Directions

Cylburn Arboretum is situated west of and adjacent to I 83. It is located on Greenspring Avenue, half a mile north of Cold Spring Lane and .2 mile south of Northern Parkway. Parking is available on the circle in front of the mansion and along the entrance road to the west.

Hike 12.3 Leakin Park

Main hike about 2.5 miles through deep, dense woods and open, grassy fields; excellent bird and wildflower trails; picnic and play areas; families and all hikers; all seasons.

Trail's Attractions

Ten years ago, the first edition of this book warned that Leakin Park was "almost certainly doomed" by the planned construction of an expressway through the heart of the park. Through litigation, area residents and park lovers delayed construction, and now the allocated money has been spent on other transportation projects. The park has apparently been spared destruction and will remain for us to enjoy.

In Leakin Park, hikers can stroll through open, grassy fields as well as along woodland paths. On the steep, wooded slopes are many springs, hidden amid the lush undergrowth. The streams are pleasant to look at but dangerously polluted by nearby "civilization." Wildflowers are abundant in spring and summer, and hordes of birds inhabit the stream valleys, woods, and wood edges. Even noisy picnickers will be treated to the enchanting songs of the wood thrush and the veery, which are abundant here. Although the

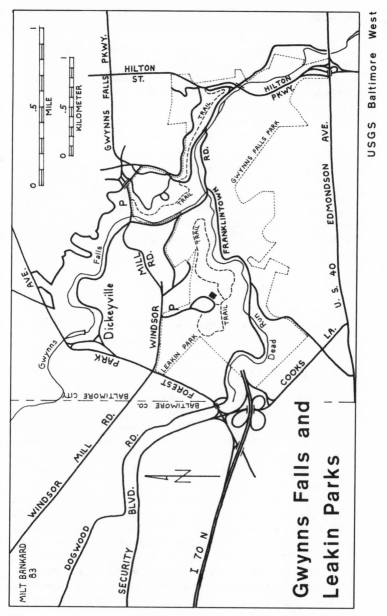

Gwynns Falls and
Leakin Parks

grounds are well kept, poison ivy is plentiful, so be careful. After heavy rains, many of the trails may be muddy. Remember, this is a city park and as such should probably not be explored alone or after dark.

Directions

Leakin Park lies in west-central Baltimore City, just inside the city line. There are many points of access to the park and many routes to reach them. One possible way from the city center, or from I 83, is via North Avenue west to Bloomingdale Road. At Bloomingdale Road, which soon becomes Windsor Mill Road, turn right (northwest) and drive 1.8 miles to the main Leakin Park entrance, which is marked on the map. There is a parking lot at the entrance to the park. A paved park road leads back to an old mansion.

There are many trails through Leakin Park. The following suggested route will take you through most of the park and to many smaller trails you may wish to explore. The main trail entrance is a dirt road to the left, about fifty yards past the mansion as you walk from the parking lot. This entrance is unattractive, as garbage has been dumped around it, but this is not representative of the rest of the trail. Take a left at the next intersection and continue downhill until you meet a trail leading to the left across the lawn downhill from the mansion. Follow this trail as it crosses the lawn and reenters the woods. Once in the woods, the trail leads downhill, veers to the left, and climbs uphill, in the vicinity of a curved stone wall. It climbs slightly for a short distance and then heads downhill, veering to the right at a major trail intersection. Cross the small bridge and continue on the main trail for about a quarter of a mile. At another major intersection, take a right and then another right near Dead Run. Follow the trail along Dead Run through the woods and overgrown field areas. Continue past the stone wall (or on top of it, if it has been raining recently), following the trail to a large clearing. This clearing includes a picnic area and is contiguous with the large lawn downhill from the mansion. You can head back to the mansion by following the lawn, heading first along the stream, then curving uphill and to the right to reach the mansion. To the left of the lawn as it leads uphill are a couple of trails, one of which parallels the lawn. You can take this trail or continue uphill on the lawn; either route will bring you back to the trail used earlier to cross the lawn below the mansion. At this trail, head back up the hill toward the road entrance. When you approach the trail entrance, instead of turning right, which would lead you back to the park road (past the small dumping area), go straight ahead. Follow this trail until it ends at an expansive clearing. Across this clearing you will see the road that will take you back to the parking area.

Hike 12.4 Gwynns Falls Park

Pleasant 1.5-mile (one-way) level woodland walk; recommended in spring and autumn.

Trail's Attractions

Gwynns Falls Park offers pleasant walks on shady, level, woodland paths. The trail runs high on the slopes of the valley, parallel to Gwynns Falls. You will see many woodland wildflowers and birds.

The park is especially pretty in the spring and fall. Summer hiking, however, is not as attractive, because of several warm weather nuisances. At this time of year, the trails in the large section of Gwynns Falls Park (near Hilton Parkway, south of Franklintown Road) are overgrown with poison ivy and are not very interesting. Better-maintained foot trails could be established here by park officials if hikers expressed enough interest. Also, the rivers are polluted and unpleasantly odoriferous in late summer. Although this is a beautiful park, it is vastly underutilized for recreation. As in most city parks, hiking alone or after dark is not recommended.

Directions

Gwynns Falls Park lies in west-central Baltimore City, just inside the city line, adjacent to Leakin Park. There are many points of access to the park and many routes to them. One way to reach the suggested trail entrance from the city center, or from I 83, is to drive west on North Avenue to Bloomingdale Road. At Bloomingdale Road (which soon becomes Windsor Mill Road), turn right (northwest) and drive for approximately 1 mile. Just past the Clifton Avenue underpass, drive down the hill to a dirt pull-out to your right just east of the bridge over Gwynns Falls. Directly across the road you will find the unmarked trail entrance. The trail, a dirt footpath, is relatively easily followed, though overgrown.

You can make a circuit hike by taking the trail all the way to Hilton Parkway. At the parkway, take a left and walk about fifty yards to Winterbourne Road. Turn left and follow this road along the park's edge to the residential area, bearing to the right as Winterbourne Road runs into Nortonia Road. Turn left on Cedric Road and left again on Chesholm Road. Follow Chesholm Road back into the park a couple of hundred yards past the road barrier, where you will meet the dirt footpath that leads back to Windsor Mill Road.

13. Some Additional Trails: Brief Remarks

Described briefly below are some fine trails that are more than an hour's drive from Baltimore.

The Appalachian Trail

The Appalachian Trail is a 2,000-mile footpath from Maine to Georgia. The trail passes through Maryland, and at its closest point (near U.S. 70, just west of Frederick, Maryland), it is less than two hours' drive from Baltimore. You can easily find the sections of the trail located in George Washington State Park and on U.S. 40A at South Mountain. For more information consult the handbooks listed in chapter 2.

The C & O Canal

Along the C & O Canal are many miles of pleasant, easy trails for families, cross-country hikers, amateur naturalists, and history buffs. For more information consult the handbooks listed in chapter 2.

Rocks State Park

Some short, interesting trails and fine rocks for climbers are features of aptly named Rocks State Park. The park is located about 30 miles northeast of Baltimore, in Harford County; to reach it take U.S. 1 and Md. 24.

Susquehanna State Park

Susquehanna State Park is an excellent park in a rocky, wooded area above the Susquehanna River, in Harford County. The park is about 35 miles northeast of Baltimore and is easily reached from I 95.

Piney Run Park

This park is administered by the Carroll County Department of Recreation and Parks—(301) 848–4500—and offers hiking trails as well as the opportunity to rent rowboats, canoes, and paddleboats. You can reach it by following Liberty Road beyond Eldersburg to White Rock Road, turning left, and proceeding south.

Trail Notes

Trail Notes

Trail Notes

Trail Notes

Trail Notes